WOMEN'S VOICES IN MAGIC

WOMEN'S VOICES IN MAGIC

BRANDY WILLIAMS

STAFFORD, ENGLAND

Women's Voices in Magic
Edited by Brandy Williams
© 2009 First edition

All rights reserved, including the right to reproduce this book, or portions thereof, in any form.

The right of individual contributors to be identified as the respective authors of this work has been asserted by them in accordance with the Copyright, Designs and Patents Act, 1988.

http://www.immanion-press.com

Cover Art:
Cover Design: Andy Bigwood
Editor: Brandy Williams
Copy Editor: Taylor Ellwood
Layout: Taylor Ellwood

Set in Book Antiqua and Algerian

Megalithica Books Edition 2009

A Megalithica Books Publication
http://www.immanion-press.com
info@immanion-press.com

8 Rowley Grove
Stafford ST17 9BJ
UK

ISBN 978-1-905713-39-4

TABLE OF CONTENTS

Introduction by Brandy Williams	8
Magical Women's History	14
Florence and the Mummy by Caroline Tully	15
The Bride of the Snake by Amy Hale	24
Hermetic Women	34
Magic and Pregnancy by Lesa Whyte	35
Enochian Motherhood by Soror Inde Seraphina	51
Are Ingredients Important? by Shellay Maughan	58
The Active and the Receptive by Kayla Block	63
Radical Feminist Alchemy by Helen Honeycutt	72
Desire - The Seeker by Kat Sanborn	76
Satanism - The Left Hand Path	80
My Life in Satanism by Venus Satanas	81
Women and the Left Hand Path by Sybil Black	89
Lilith, Babalon, and Sexuality	102
The Rose of Sharon by Alison More	103
Every Time You Play the Red by Kirsten Brown	114
Whore by Leni Hester	119
The Female Kink Magician by Lupa	126
Culture Bearers	136
Words Beneath the Willow by Teresa Garcia	137
Cove Witches and Curanderas by Byron Ballard	148
What I Hold in my Hand by Kris Leet	152
Speaking as a Woman	158
The Accidental Magician by Grace Victoria Swann	159
His Mother's Whole Body Heals by Erynn Rowan Laurie	167
Where Do I Go From Here? by Jaymi Elford	174
The Feminist Adept by Brandy Williams	181
Three Chapters from a Magical Life by Mordant Carnival	190
Conclusion by Brandy Williams	195

INTRODUCTION

Why collect an anthology of women's magical work? What difference does it make whether the magician is a woman or a man? What is the point of emphasizing the gender of the writer - isn't the point the work itself?

Women are vitally involved in the magical communities. There are women Ceremonial Magicians, women Satanists, women sex magicians. But the world does not always know that - it still comes as a surprise to many that women participate, and in such large numbers. It still comes as a surprise when women speak our experiences of these magics.

As I write this I am listening to an eight-hundred-year-old song:

> *A chantar m'er de so q'ieu no volria*
> *tant me rancur de lui cui sui amia*
> *car eu l'am mais que nuilla re que sia*
> *vas lui no.m val merces e cortesia*
> *ni ma beltatz ni mos pretz ni mos sens*
> *c'atressi.m sui enganada e trahia*
> *com d'egresser, s'ieu fos desavinens.*

> I must give voice to that which I do not want to sing,
> I have such bitter pain from my friend;
> I love him more than all the world,
> yet my mercy and courtesy do not aid me,
> nor my beauty, nor my name, nor my brilliance -
> I am deceived and betrayed
> as I would deserve if I were unworthy.

This song comes to us from the twelfth century, written by a trobairitz we know as La Comtesse de Dia, the Countess of Dia. We do not have her proper name. Of the handful of troubadour texts written by women, it is the only one for which the music also survives. Musicians perform and record this song over and over, partly because it is the only surviving female voice from this genre of song, and partly because of its tone – the reluctance to sing, the grace with which she bears betrayal, and the injustice of being held less worthy than she knows herself to be.

A woman may not own the story of her life. *A chantar m'er de so q'ieu no volria* is significant not only because so few troubairitz songs survive, but because the singer seizes the right to speak in a tradition which casts the lady as the musician's inspiration. The role of muse places the woman's life under the artist's shadow, whether or not she is an artist herself. Carolyn Heilbrun points to "F. Scott Fitzgerald's assumption that he had the right to the life of his wife, Zelda, as his artistic property. She went mad..." (Heilbrun 1988). In the last century Anais Nin rebelled against Henry Miller's demand that she reserve her life for his material, instead journaling her life and then publishing the journals.

History records the deeds of men. We hear about great battles and kings, the deeds of priests and male saints, male artists of genius, and male musicians who were passionate lovers. Women achieve great accomplishments as well, ruling and fighting, praying and painting, singing and loving, but these stories drop out of history.

In the last several decades women have worked to recover these stories, collecting them in great volumes, *A History of Women*, *Women's History of the World*, the *Uppity Women* series. These collections serve as a resource for later historians who can re-situate them in general histories of a place and time, so that women's history is not a separate subject, but women are again represented in history. This is an ongoing project. Even today, despite the massive information available about women in, say, ancient Egypt, and the numerous volumes written about them, it is still possible for an educated woman to say to me that there were no women who ruled Egypt, and for a male operative magician to express surprise to me that women held active roles in the temples.

Western philosophers from Aristotle through Kant to Lacan and Freud have argued that women are deformed men, unable to reason, and therefore unable to speak. Only in the last few decades have women philosophers struggled to find a way to reply to this, to establish a philosophical understanding of woman that does not define her as an absence of power, and in particular, to offer an image of the whole woman who is able to reason and to speak. It is still today very unusual to find a history of philosophy which includes mention of any women at all. Like the general histories of women's lives, Sister Prudence Allen's *Concept of Woman* series gathers the philosophical writings of women in the Western tradition (Allen 1985, 2002). These writings also serve as a resource

Introduction

to include women in the Western conversation about the meaning of life, and how we know what we know.

This assumption at the deepest root of culture, that women cannot think, surfaces in the way women are expected and permitted to learn. In the 1980s a group of woman sociologists interviewed women to discover how they grew into the exercise of reason. Belenky, Clinchy, Goldberger and Tarule were disciples of William Perry (Belenky 1986). He had interviewed college men to trace an arc of intellectual discovery. He found a young man moved from a dualistic understanding (me/you, right/wrong, black/white) through challenging authority into understanding that truth is relative and finally growing into a position of authority himself.

The four researchers made a different choice than Perry, to interview women, and not just women attending college but women from all walks of life. They discovered that girls began to learn from a different position than Perry's young men. They often began from silence, the inability to speak at all. Only when a woman moved from this position could she begin to articulate opinions received from authority, then learn to trust her own experience, before maturing into an integrated understanding of herself as part of a community of reasoning women and men.

We lose our voices at twelve. Carol Lee Flinders movingly describes the connections she made with girls in her own community after the death of Polly Klass. Death is the ultimate silencing, and points to the violence involved in denying the right to speak. The transition from girlhood to adulthood in contemporary Western culture is the moment when exploration stops, confidence turns to diffidence, and then to silence. Flinders offers models from other cultures which help girls make the transition from child to adult. She points to women's need to support one another in speaking. She says, "Confide in one another. Listen to one another. See how strong you are *together*." She quotes Carolyn Heilbrun: "We must begin to tell the truth, in groups, to one another" (Flinders 1998).

Women talk differently to each other than we do to men. In numerous cultures women have a separate language from that of the men in that culture. This is true of American women today. Deborah Tannen documented the differing speaking styles of women and men. She found that men establish hierarchy through conversation, taking turns speaking, while women talk simultaneously, overlapping each other in a supportive style. These observations apply to single-sex groups. When men speak with women, men experience women's overlapping talk as interrupting rather than supportive. In mixed-sex groups, men's style dominates, with women deferring the floor to men (Tannen 1991).

Women speaking together overlap in cooperative language. In this introduction I have assembled a literary community - La Comtesse de Dia; Heilbrun; Allen; Belenky, Clinchy, Goldberger and Tarule; Tannen; Flinders - to provide a context for what I wish to say. Over and over again these women bring me back to the understanding that women's voices are silenced, and that when we support one another, we can speak.

Because men take the speaking floor and women cede it to them, because women lose our stories, and because Western women are not expected or permitted to speak at all, it is important to make spaces where only women are allowed to speak. It can take a woman a long time to find her voice. She must feel safe in the environment where she is encouraged to speak. She must know that her story will not be used as raw material for someone else's story. Her speech may be hesitant at first and require validation - is it okay that I say this? Are you listening to me?

This isn't true for every woman. There are many strong women who come out of the gate speaking in no uncertain terms about our own experiences and our own reasoned conclusions. Strong women may resent the implication that we require assistance to speak, or that our work is fundamentally different from that of the men around us. Because traditional women's community provides support to the needs of men, of families, and of communities before supporting the needs of the women who make it, strong women may have left the community of women to move out into the world and be recognized for our accomplishments. It is as challenging to bring these women into conversation with other women as it is to encourage silenced women to speak. Of course the community benefits from that strength. It also happens that when we do enter into woman-only space we discover that we do not always have to be strong, and we find ourselves speaking in a different voice and saying different things. Our strength can be augmented and sustained by the strength of the people around us.

When women do gather together to speak, what we say may or may not be different than what men or mixed groups would say. Women's topics are expected to center on the concerns of the body and of family - being sexually attractive to men, giving birth, and raising children. In magical terms we are sometimes cast as the soror mysticae, the assistant to the male magician on his journey toward wholeness, and we are expected to embody the Divine Feminine, mysterious, inspirational, and, yes, largely silent.

Of course only women can speak about the experience of pregnancy and how the cycles of fertility affect our magical energy. But that is not the only or even the primary interest of woman magicians. Women can and do speak about the experience of being cast into the lesser gender, of being held to be less worthy than we know ourselves to be, even in the magical communities where each of us is striving to recognize and express our own power. That also may not be our first concern. We are in the magical communities, building and defining them, because we derive great strength from them. They are our inspirations, our guides, our paths, our homes. Some women's magical writings could only have been written by a woman. Other writings may not be distinguishable as a woman's voice at all. Women are not interested in a subset of magic, but in magic itself.

This collection of women's essays about our own magical work serves the same function as other histories or collections of women's writings. It presents women as essential and integral parts of the magical communities in which we work, in the past, and in the present. It provides a place to speak, however loudly or quietly, about whatever topic interests the writer. The contributors do not speak in a common voice, or even in a special woman's voice, but from individual and unique perspectives. Collected together they remind us to include women in our philosophy, our history, our communities, and our understanding of magic. They form a literary community encouraging every woman to speak and to pursue any magical path.

REFERENCES

Allen, Sister Prudence (1985). *The Concept of Woman: The Aristotelian Revolution, 750 B.C. – A.D. 1250*. Grand Rapids: William B. Eerdmans Publishing Company, 1985.

Allen, Sister Prudence (2002). *The Concept of Woman, Volune II: the Early Humanist Reformation, 1250-1500, Part 1*. Grand Rapids: William B. Eerdmans Publishing Company, 2002.

Allen, Sister Prudence (2002). *The Concept of Woman, Volune II: the Early Humanist Reformation, 1250-1500, Part 2*. Grand Rapids: William B. Eerdmans Publishing Company, 2002.

Belenky, Mary, Blythe Clinchy, Nancy Goldberger and Jill Tarule (1986). *Women's Ways of Knowing, The Development of Self, Voice and Mind*. New York: Basic Books.

Heilbrun, Carolyn (1988). *Writing a Woman's Life*. New York: Ballantine Books.

Flinders, Carol Lee (1998). *At the Root of This Longing, Reconciling a Spiritual Hunger and a Feminist Thirst*. New York: Harper Collins.

Tannen, Deborah (1991). *You Just Don't Understand, Women and Men in Conversation*. New York: HarperCollins.

MAGICAL WOMEN'S HISTORY

At the beginning of the modern era women entered the magical lodges as full participants and took leadership roles in those groups, including the Golden Dawn and O.T.O. lodges and their offshoots. Women today spotlight the contributions of these women, as Amy Hale's biography of Ithell Colquohon, and re-assess their contributions, as in Caroline Tully's critique of Florence Farr's Egyptology. Retelling their biographies keeps these women in the historical record. They form part of our magical heritage and the continuity of what we do as magical women.

FLORENCE AND THE MUMMY
CAROLINE TULLY

Born in England in 1860, Florence Farr entered a world steeped in Spiritualism, Theosophy, and Hermeticism. A professional actress from the age of twenty-two, by the time she was thirty Farr would be initiated into the Hermetic Order of the Golden Dawn in which she attained the position of national leadership by 1897. As a successful Golden Dawn initiate it was to be expected that Farr would become fascinated by Egyptian religion, considering the large part it played in Golden Dawn ceremonies as well as Egypt's ubiquitous presence in Late Victorian London exhibitions. In addition to assuming responsibility for the entire Order in Britain, Farr composed and performed complex rituals to Egyptian deities, lectured publicly on Egyptological subjects, and wrote two Egyptianising plays, and after resigning from the Golden Dawn in 1902, was conducting her own 'Egyptian' initiations by 1903. Like her immediate superior and mentor in the Golden Dawn, Samuel Liddell 'MacGregor' Mathers, Farr utilised the British Museum as a place for both artistic inspiration and study. It was while researching material for her book, *Egyptian Magic*, in the British Museum in 1895 that Farr made contact with what she described as 'an Egyptian Adept' whom she would subsequently introduce to a secret group formed within the Golden Dawn.

The identity of Farr's 'Egyptian Adept' is contested. On the one hand, friends of hers to whom she left a wooden 'shrine' in which an Egyptian being allegedly dwelt claim that its name was Nemkheftka whereas on the other hand, eye-witnesses report that the name of the entity was Mut-em-menu. Either way, this 'Adept' was a long-dead ancient Egyptian that Florence obviously felt perfectly comfortable about 'speaking' with. The idea that one could converse with the dead was a staple of Victorian Spiritualism and it was a cornerstone of the Hermeticism that imbued the Golden Dawn that all knowledge is obtained through revelation, not reason. Ancient Egyptians had a habit of manifesting themselves to kindred spirits in the 1890s and even London journalists reviewing Late Victorian exhibits of Egyptian antiquities were liable to 'reanimate and evoke the people of the past in a quasi-psychic way... as if through a medium.' (Montserrat 1998). Consequently it was not at all unusual for Farr to believe that she could receive information through a discarnate entity she met in the British Museum.

Both Nemkheftka and Mut-em-menu were (and are) part of the Egyptian collection in the British Museum. Nemkheftka—actually Ne**n**kheftka—is a painted limestone statue of a provincial official from Deshasha, dating to the 5th Dynasty, around 2400 BCE, at the height of the Old Kingdom. The statue was acquired by the British Museum in 1897, so 'Nemkheftka' could not have been the 'personality' Florence was in contact with in 1895, although it seems that he did fulfil that role after 1901. 'Mut-em-menu', a coffined mummy acquired by the British Museum in 1835, is a likelier candidate for Farr's 'Egyptian Adept' at this time. Like other museum attendees, Farr would have been under the impression that Mutemmenu was 'a lady of the college of the God Amen-Ra at Thebes', (Budge 1898), however we now know that this description is only half correct. While the coffin is indeed that of Mutemmenu, a Chantress of Amun, dating from the 19th (1295–1186 BCE) or 20th (1186–1069 BCE) Dynasties, the mummy in the coffin dates from the Roman period (30 BCE–395 CE) and is actually that of a man whose wrappings are padded and swathed so as to imitate feminine features such as breasts and rounded thighs.

It is understandable that in the 1890s this mummy would be taken at face value to have been female and Farr obviously deemed Mutemmenu a satisfactory link with the authentic Egyptian past. Fellow Golden Dawn member William Butler Yeats re-created Florence's British Museum experiences in his unfinished novel *The Speckled Bird* where the hero, Michael Hearne (Yeats), accompanied by Maclagan (Mathers), was to meet a certain woman at the Britsh Museum who is later discovered meditating 'with her eyes half closed on a seat close to the Mut-em-menu mummy case.' She is not to be disturbed because, according to Maclagan, 'she is doubtless conversing with Mut-em-menu' who was, among other things, describing Farr's past incarnations.

Florence went to Paris in 1896 to confer with MacGregor and Moina Mathers about her 'Egyptian Adept', a drawing of whom she had previously sent them. MacGregor Mathers agreed that because the Egyptian had responded appropriately to signs that Florence had shown her, she was indeed 'one of the $8°=3°'$, making her one of the Secret Chiefs. He subsequently gave permission for Farr to form a group with higher degree members of the Golden Dawn to 'work with' the Egyptian.

Mathers also suggested that Farr should make offerings to Mutemmenu. Instead of researching ancient Egyptian funerary offerings, Farr chose the Hermetic method of obtaining knowledge through revelation to discern exactly what kind of offerings would be most suitable. She assembled a small group of Golden Dawn higher degree members who, through clairvoyant means, would make contact with Mutemmenu. According to Florence's transcript of the vision the group found themselves:

> [In a] chamber ... measuring about 4 feet, walls white, a bed with Lions Heads at the Top and Lions feet at the bottom ornamenting the posts a coverlet with stripes coloured White, Red & Green, the center ornamented with a Double Phoenix head elaborately worked up, a window at the left hand of the Chamber rather high up: it appears to be a cubicle opening out—into an Adytum without a roof opening into a court with water and a fountain playing, it is a Temple on the mainland and not on an Island. The place is very hot and the sun most powerful.
>
> She is dressed in white with a Lamen under her dress ... She was the keeper of Documents connected with the Mystic Order and was in a position of authority, so much so that some of her enemies plotted for her death and downfall: but before they could kill her, she died of a plague or disease generated after a Battle had been fought, and thus was not killed by the plotting of her enemies.
>
> The Box [Florence had had a wooden box made as a shrine for this being] in which I have placed her should be painted white, preferably with coloured designs from the Egyptian temples of a suitable character, and a wand should be placed therein the height of the Box coloured white with a Blue Lotus Top, green petals outside and blue in—she would prefer a Phoenix Wand, but a Lotus one is better for her. [A Phoenix wand is used by by ritual participants impersonating Egyptian deities in the Neophyte Ceremony and the Lotus wand is assigned to members of the Zelator Adeptus Minor Grade.]
>
> She will not be of so much use to me in my mental Studies as in Magical Physical work.

> She appeared to be lame in one of her legs having had an accident to her hip bone when very young, and on account of that, her Parents gave her a golden anklet of a snake pattern to wear, this anklet had a proportion of Tin in it as a Physician had given instructions to have this done—so as to ease her of her complaint, which went a certain extent to accomplishing it.
>
> In appearance she is Tall and Slender, born under Leo, with Black Hair and Eyes and Face, Almond Eyes and pointed chin dressed in white with a jewelled girdle round her waist and a jewelled head Dress.
> I should place a white water lily before her in her present position ... [End of transcript]. (Greer 1995)

The key point in this vision is the use to which Mutemmenu can be to Farr: this ancient Egyptian contact will be of use in her 'Magical Physical work.' Farr assumes that Mutemmenu, as a 'Priestess of the temple of Amon at Thebes' has 'magical' knowledge. According to her book *Egyptian Magic* written the same year, no doubt with help from 'Mutemmenu', Farr conflated Egyptian temple cult with 'magic', believed in 'Egyptian Mysteries' and a 'priestly school of wisdom', an idea deriving not from ancient Egypt but from Terrasson's *Life of Sethos* of 1731, a fictional work describing elaborate ancient Egyptian initiations which would have influenced the Golden Dawn via Freemasonry. In addition, Farr opined that 'there is every reason to suppose that only those [ancient Egyptians] who had received some grade of initiation were mummified.' (Farr 1896). The type of 'initiation' Farr was familiar with was the 'magical' initiation of the Golden Dawn. What a stroke of luck then, that Mutemmenu happened to be a mummy.

Not only was she a mummified initiate of high degree but Mutemmenu was also a bona fide priestess. The Golden Dawn was unusual in being a Masonic-style organisation that admitted women. Believing that, in the words of Moina Mathers, the 'object of this school was similar to the foundation in ancient times of centers for the Celebration of the Mysteries,' (Owen 2004), the women of the group took their roles as 'priestesses of the mysteries' seriously. High Priestess of Isis, Moina, explained her obviously Bachofen-inspired ideas about women's sacred roles thus:

Caroline Tully

> The idea of the Priestess is at the root of all ancient beliefs ... [and] finds her force in her alliance with the sympathetic energies of Nature ... Woman is the magician born of Nature by reason of her great natural sensibility and of her instructive sympathy with ...subtle energies ... of the air, the earth, the fire and water. (Lees 1900)

Farr was the only Order member to be in direct contact with an ancient Egyptian priestess who, according to her invented biography, was also an Adept of high degree. Farr evidently assumed that both she and Mutemmenu were speaking the same religious language. We know Mutemmenu was a New Kingdom Chantress of Amun from 19th or 20th Dynasty Thebes. Would a late nineteenth century CE British member of the Golden Dawn have anything in common (besides having been her in a past life) with a Chantress of Amun?

If by 'Chantress' the Egyptian term *shemayet*, musician, is meant—which was a title used by large numbers of New Kingdom elite women—then yes, Mutemmenu and Farr had something in common as Farr was musical and particularly interested in the idea of sacred sound. The title 'musician' in the New Kingdom specifically referred to music-making in the divine cult. Mutemmenu probably served in the cult of Amun, his wife Mut or his son Khons as a musician, utilising a sistrum and shaking a *menit* necklace, tambourine or clappers and singing hymns. (Interestingly, the Roman-era mummy that accompanied the Mutemmenu coffin is believed to have been a dancer who performed at religious ceremonies or banquets.) *Shemayet* was the second most common title found for women on the Theban tombs. This plethora of New Kingdom female musicians indicates that there was widespread participation in this cult role, a consequence of which would have been a decrease in the status of female priests. Mutemmenu probably had less responsibility in her cult than Farr did in Golden Dawn.

If Mutemmenu's main cultic task was music-making, it is no wonder then that she was not very helpful when it came to the intricacies of ancient Egyptian magic. Florence's book on Egyptian magic is an unashamedly Hermetic interpretation of parts of the New Kingdom *Book of the Dead*, the *Harris Magical Papyrus* (19th-20th Dynasties) and the *Bruce Codex* (fifth century CE), accompanied by an exegesis on ancient Egyptian kingship, priesthood, 'mysteries', 'initiation', and reincarnation. Throughout the book Farr refers to *theurgy*, citing the third century CE Iamblichus, obviously under the impression that Egyptian 'magic' was the same from the Pharaonic era to Late Antiquity. Farr's disregard for chronology means that she approached her topic with a 'kaleidoscope technique ... bringing together inspirations across space and time.' (Meskell 1995) This is also evident in her approach to physical ritual in which components from Medieval Kabbala, the *Key of Solomon* and Hebrew and Greek are mixed with the sixty-fourth chapter of the *Book of the Dead*. Farr must have expected Mutemmenu to be knowledgeable about all the periods of Egyptian history including her own.

That Farr's Egyptology was abysmal is evidenced by Professor of Egyptology, Flinders Petrie's assessment of her booklet about Egypt that she sent him for review in 1897. He read it and responded that the British public would not 'swallow' its 'doses'. Not deterred by academic criticism or her own lack of Egyptological qualifications, Farr was still blithely lecturing away on Egypt in 1901. According to fellow Golden Dawn member, Arthur Edward Waite, who attended one of her lectures:

> She knows, however a good deal of her subject—or so she impresses me—and hence it follows that (1) it is not necessary, or perhaps even desirable, to go to Egypt in order to be learned in things Egyptian; and (2) that you can know much of antiquity without being able to construe its dead languages.

Waite's comment sounds tongue-in-cheek yet within two years he would undergo initiation into Farr's Egyptian Rite. In the meantime Farr continued to obtain her knowledge of Egypt through Hermetic revelation rather than referring to Egyptological literature. It was not surprising then that her plays, *The Beloved of Hathor* and *The Shrine of the Golden Hawk* performed in 1902 at the Egyptian Hall, 'England's home of mystery and arcana' in Piccadilly, displayed wildly imprecise time periods and historical inaccuracies, despite the availability of Manetho's chronology.

The first decade of the twentieth century saw Mutemmenu replaced in the role of Egyptian Adept by Nemkheftka who would maintain this position until Farr emigrated to Ceylon in 1912. According to Edmund and Dorothea Hunter, to whom Farr entrusted the wooden shrine that was once Mutemmenu's—and now Nemkheftka's—home, not only was Nemkheftka her new Egyptian contact, he was also her 'Ka'—the Egyptian manifestation of a person's vital force. Florence considered the Ka to be the celestial double of the material person, the real Ego or Self, whose mission was to grow and develop through 'celestial evolution' just as physical bodies evolved in the material world. She seems to have picked an Egyptian from the wrong time period for this task however, as no one in the Old Kingdom except the Pharaoh had a Ka. All the same, the 'shrine' was held in great reverence by Dorothea Hunter who instructed her heir that if ever it fell into neglect or was subjected to disrespect, it should be reverently burned.

In her quest for ancient wisdom Farr combined the classic Spiritualist technique of contact with the dead with the typical denial of historical discovery, love of 'rejected knowledge', and reliance on revelation espoused by Hermeticism. In her fervent desire to understand the components and manifest the role of authentic priestess, Farr biographised a mummy, mixed anachronistic definitions of 'magic' with ancient Egyptian cult practice, and lumped vastly different Egyptian eras into a homogenous magical past. Like her teachers Moina and MacGregor Mathers, Farr believed in the supernatural beings which whom she presumed to interact, derived aesthetic pleasure from ancient Egyptian literature and material culture, as well as social credibility, seeming an authority on the topic from the perspective of other amateurs. Deeply entrenched in a Hermetic worldview, instead of modifying her beliefs about ancient Egypt in the face of scientific discovery, Farr co-opted 'Egypt' into the project of the pursuit of Hermetic wisdom.

REFERENCES

Andrews, Carol A.R., (1985). "Introduction." In Faulkner, Raymond O. (trans). *The Ancient Egyptian Book of the Dead*. New York: Macmillan.

Budge, E.A. Wallis (1898). *A Guide to the First and Second Egyptian Rooms. Predynastic Antiquities, Mummies, Mummy-Cases, and Other Objects Connected with the Funeral Rites of the Ancient Egyptians*. London: British Museum, Dept of Egyptian and Assyrian Antiquities.

Farr, Florence and Shakespear, Olivia. *The Beloved of Hathor and The Shrine of the Golden Hawk*. (n.p. n.d).

Farr, Florence (1896, 1982). *Egyptian Magic*. Wellingborough: The Aquarian Press, 1896, 1982.

Frankfurter, David (1998). *Religion in Roman Egypt: Assimilation and Resistance*. Princeton. Princeton University Press.
Georgoudi, Stella (1992). "Creating a Myth of Matriarchy." In Duby, Georges; Perrot, Michelle; and Pantel, Pauline Schmitt. (Eds), *A History of Women in the West: From Ancient Goddesses to Christian Saints*. Cambridge. Belknap Press.
Gilbert, R.A. (1997). *The Golden Dawn Scrapbook*. York Beach: Samuel Weiser.
Greer, Mary Katherine (1995). *Women of the Golden Dawn: Rebels and Priestesses*. Rochester: Park Street Press.
Hornung, Erik (2001). *The Secret Lore of Egypt: Its Impact on the West*. Ithaca: Cornell University Press.
Johnson, Josephine (1975). *Florence Farr: Bernard Shaw's 'New Woman'*. Gerrards Cross: Colin Smythe.
Johnston, Sarah Iles (2004). (Ed). *Religions in the Ancient World: A Guide*. Cambridge: Belknap Press.
King, Karen L (2003). *What is Gnosticism?* Cambridge: Belknap Press, 2003.
Lees, Frederic (1900). "Isis Worship in Paris: Conversations with the Hierophant Rameses and the High Priestess Anari." in *The Humanitarian* 16: 2, 82–87.
McDermott, Bridget (2006). *Death in Ancient Egypt*. Phoenix Mill: Sutton Publishing Ltd.
Meskell, Lynn (1995). "Goddesses, Gimbutas and 'New Age' Archaeology." In *Antiquity* 69, 74-86.
Montserrat, Dominic (1998). "Unidentified Human Remains: Mummies and the erotics of biography." In Montserrat, Domenic (Ed.) *Changing Bodies, Changing Meanings: Studies on the human body in antiquity*. London: Routledge, 162–197.
Morenz, Siegfried (1973). *Egyptian Religion*. Ithaca: Cornell University Press.
Owen, Alex (1989). *The Darkened Room: Women, Power, and Spiritualism in Late Victorian England*. Chicago: University of Chicago Press.
Owen, Alex (2004). *The Place of Enchantment: British Occultism and the Culture of the Modern*. Chicago: University of Chicago Press.
Putnam, James (1993). *Mummy*. London: Dorling Kindersley.
Regardie, Israel (1990). *The Complete Golden Dawn System of Magic*. Volume Eight. Scottsdale: New Falcon Publications.
Ritner, Robert Kriech (1993). *The Mechanics of Ancient Egyptian Magical Practice*. Studies in Ancient Oriental Civilization.

Number 54. Chicago. The Oriental Institute of the University of Chicago.

Robins, Gay (1993). *Women in Ancient Egypt.* London: British Museum Press.

Terrasson, Jean (1732). *Life of Séthos.* (trans. Thomas Lediard). London: J. Walthoe, 1732.

Toomey, Deirdre, ed. (1997). *Yeats and Women.* Second edition. Houndmills: Macmillan Press.

Watterson, Barbara (1991). *Women in Ancient Egypt.* New York: St. Martin's Press.

Yeats, William Butler (1976). *The Speckled Bird.* Ed. William H. O'Donnell. Toronto: McClelland and Steward.

Images

See image of Nenkheftka: http://tinyurl.com/q7a3km
See mummy from Mutemmenu coffin: http://tinyurl.com/of2q8d

Biography

Caroline Tully has been involved in various forms of contemporary Paganism, Witchcraft and Ceremonial Magick since 1984. Formally initiated as a Witch in 1985, she subsequently became a Scion of the Church of All Worlds in 1992 and joined the Ordo Templi Orientis in 1993. In 1999 Caroline's path was significantly transformed through, on the one hand, the discovery of Pagan Reconstructionism (the practice of historically-correct ancient Pagan religions) and on the other, the publication of Ronald Hutton's investigation into the historical claims of modern Pagan Witchcraft, Triumph of the Moon. In 2004 Caroline enrolled at Melbourne University in a Postgraduate Diploma in Classics and Archaeology in order to assess, from an academic standpoint, the claims to historicity of the Neo-Pagan founders she had encountered both through literature and in person. Her major areas of investigation are the Hermetic Order of the Golden Dawn and its offshoots, and the form of Stregheria influenced by Charles Godfrey Leland's Aradia or the Gospel of the Witches. Caroline has been published in many international Pagan publications and has contributed to several Pagan anthologies.

THE BRIDE OF THE SNAKE: A BRIEF INTRODUCTION TO THE MAGIC OF ITHELL COLQUHOUN
AMY HALE

Regardless of her gender, Ithell Colquhoun may have been one of the most prolific and creative occult practitioners of the 20th century. Her art and her life were magic, as they provided the conduit and communications for other worlds and to the Gods. In this essay I hope to provide an introduction to the life and work of Ithell Colquhoun, as well as to explore various facets of both her Hermetic and her Pagan magical practices.

Ithell Colquhoun was born in India in 1906, as her father was serving in the military there. As a young girl she went to Cheltenham Ladies School, and later studied art at the Slade. She took a very early interest in biology, and many of her early notebooks were filled with highly detailed representations of flowers and plants. The study of plants and flowers was a theme to which she returned many times during her life, in her painting and drawing and in her writing, frequently using plants as visual metaphors for eroticism.

Her Approach to Surrealism

Ithell first encountered surrealism when she studied in Paris from 1931-33. She later visited the international Surrealist Exposition in London in 1936, and it was clear within the next two years that Surrealism was starting to impact her work more directly, primarily influenced by her exposure to Salvador Dali. In 1939 she visited Andre Breton in Paris, and started working with automatic techniques in her writing and painting. By 1940 she was identifying herself as a Surrealist, and this is a label to which she firmly adhered for the entirety of her life. Also in 1940 there was a split in the British surrealist movement. The Belgian surrealist ELT Mesens took over as figurehead, and decreed that no one involved with the British Surrealist movement would publish or belong to any group that was not in service of Surrealism. Ithell refused to sever her occult ties and relinquish her interests, and as a result she publicly separated from British surrealism. Unlike many of her Surrealist counterparts in Britain, Ithell did not view Surrealism as part of a wider political or socialist agenda, although she clearly believed in its revolutionary capacity.

Colquhoun's Surrealist body of work was wide-ranging and extensive. Although Surrealism tends to be associated most frequently with the visual arts, particularly those of a type which are highly representational and fantastic, it is important to stress that Surrealism was initially a movement expressed through writing. Surrealism was and is not a style, it is a philosophy, and a worldview. Most Surrealists enacted their experiments in poetry, prose, visual arts, and performance. As such, to consider Colquhoun primarily as a visual artist, would be to diminish her own personal Surrealist project. She was prolific with just about everything she did. She created thousands of pieces of visual art, wrote, published and performed hundreds of poems, wrote several novels, two of which were unpublished, three travel guides, one of which was unpublished, radio dramas, commentaries, and quite a large number of esoteric related essays. Although not all of her work would be identified as explicitly Surrealist, she would have identified that as a primary current within her life, and most important to her was the link between the Surreal and the Fantastic.

Colquhoun frequently claimed throughout her life that she was the only true Surrealist left working in Britain. She may have made this claim because the ways in which her own work reflected the automatism and the preeminent position of the unconscious that was key to the works of Andre Breton and many other Surrealists, notably Dali. However, much of her visual and written work diverged from the Surrealists and should be considered primarily esoteric art, because she does not emphasize chance and open interpretation to the same degree. Colquhoun used both automatic methods and Hermetic methods to create works which simultaneously drew on subconscious elements and dream imagery, yet also were primed with specific intent, coded by the artist according to Hermetic principles.

Colquhoun demonstrated a very early interest in the occult and in alchemy, and it was probably this that made her interest in Surrealism a very natural match. Her cousin was Edward Langford Garstin, who was a member of The Golden Dawn, and friends with MacGregor Mathers. He was also secretary of the GRS Mead's Quest society that Colquhoun joined in 1928. It would be no underestimation to argue for the preeminence of the occult in Ithell's body of work. It was very clearly an overriding preoccupation from a relatively young age; her earliest writings on alchemy, Kabbalah and Enochian magic, dated from the 1920s. The degree to which genuine occultism was an influence in the wider Surrealist movement is debatable. I believe that there is a difference between employing occult tropes and symbols in artistic creation and having a commitment to a sustained esoteric practice. The primary connection between Surrealism in general and occult processes is to be found in automatism, which was a key feature of Ithell's work, and according to Andre Breton's first Surrealist manifesto the defining feature of Surrealism itself (Polizzotti 209). Automatism was somewhat inspired by, yet different from, mediumistic automatism. The source of automatic images in Surrealism was not believed to be spirits, but the psyche itself releasing repressed desires and impulses. Automatic writing was in many ways close to stream of consciousness, while automatic art techniques were based on seemingly random applications of paint to canvas or paper to see what emerged. Other forms of automatism included collage, found objects or found poems, frottage or rubbings, and a number of other techniques designed to incorporate elements of chance and play into the creative process. Surrealists also embraced the works of Freud, dream states, hysteria, games of chance and madness. They looked for freedom from logical processes and direct, unmediated access to the unconscious. Surrealists believed that automatic processes would generate a sense of randomness out of which one could explore the workings of the subconscious. In 1941, Breton noted that the two primary visual forms of Surrealist expression were based either in automatism or the recording of dream like images, but said that automatism was closer to true Surrealist method.

Additionally, Surrealists drew on a variety of occult symbols. Andre Breton's references to alchemy in the 1929 Second Surrealist Manifesto and also to the "occultation" of Surrealism are sometimes interpreted by art historians as examples of adoption of a Hermetic position (Polizzotti 325). It is evident that a number of individual artists had occult, mystical and mythological themes in their works. Leonora Carrington and Max Ernst, for example, frequently used alchemical symbolism such as eggs and alembics in their paintings and written work, while the image of the hermaphrodite was seen as a Surrealist ideal, as well as an occult ideal. For the core of male surrealists in the movement the hermaphroditic ideal was to be gained through the channel of the Muse, or conjunction with the female creative principle. We can hypothesize that women associated with Surrealism had their own interpretation of the hermaphrodite, and the work of Claude Cahun might be of interest in this regard (Ades 1980). We also know that Surrealists were reading writers of the French occult revival, notably Eliphas Levi, and of course had a love of tarot cards, of which Surrealists created a variety of decks over the years.

A primary question then would be the degree to which Colquhoun's interest in the occult and her use of occult symbols and techniques in her Surrealism was similar to other Surrealists, and the ways in which it was different. Because she considered herself to be engaging in magical acts, and because she believed in the objective reality of the figures and concepts with which she was working, her use of them was both divinatory and ritualistic. She was consistently working with otherworldly realms, and although she was using automatic processes, she was also directing the symbolism and the colors for specific ends. Surrealist scholars such as Dawn Ades have argued that Colquhoun's primary method of Surrealist working was the highly representational dream image, mostly inspired by her interest in Salvador Dali, but Colquhoun would argue that automatic processes were at the basis of her Surrealist practice, and for that reason she remained consistent with the directives and programs of the early continental Surrealists (Ades 1980, Colquhoun 1981).

What seems to be a primary difference in Ithell's use of Surrealist techniques is that her conception of the spaces one would contact using automatic processes would be inhabited by specific beings, and reached using a variety of esoteric languages. She did not just use these techniques to see what came of them with her mind in a state unfettered by logic and rationality, or to explore subconscious desires. These other planes had things to communicate to her and as such her art was part of her road to enlightenment, invocation and ritual. For instance, she interpreted the four major automatic processes as corresponding to the four elements, fire to fumage (which is developing figures from a canvas or paper which has been previously smoked), water to parsemage (which is when charcoal or pastel are floated on water and then gently apply to paper), air to techniques where things are blown on paper, such as charcoal, paint or pastel, and decalcomania, where prints are either transferred or superimposed from one surface to another, to earth. Therefore, when she chose which process she would use, she was in some way prescribing intent or focus into the artistic outcome (Colquhoun 1949).

Although many of the early Surrealists promoted the idea that their works were created by chance, randomness, and pure access to the unconscious, of course that is not completely true. Any of Breton's works which may have been guided by automatic principles were also guided by aesthetics, and in the end editing. Words went together because they sounded good, or the imagery was intriguing. The automatic process may have started off a painting, but it was later shaped by the creator to bring out more of a recognizable meaning for both artist and audience. Colquhoun worked the same way, but she frequently would use as her starting point colors or a text which already had some sort of personal esoteric meaning to her, and would be useful for further contemplation for invocation. For instance, she developed a set of "found poems" from Wallace Budges' translation of the Egyptian Book of the Dead. On reading them, they are not so much found poems as invocations, and rituals to be done at cardinal points using Egyptian symbolism. They were not random, nothing ever is, what she was doing was using her conception of the mental and psychic space one opens up to create something sacred from the profane. Similarly, she wrote a series of poems designed to reflect the polarities of male and female and to emphasize duality. They were titled "Poems of He and She", and they were lists of masculine and feminine nouns taken from a Gaelic grammar. The idea of her automatic poetry was to bring the order from the random, but order that was ultimately instructive about the nature of the universe, and in this case alchemical duality.

The Hermetic and Alchemical Current

Although Ithell clearly showed Hermetic and alchemical influences in her art from a very early age, her involvement in occult organizations really emerged in the 1950s, after her divorce from Toni Del Renzio in 1947. Until this time, Ithell was much more integrated into both Modernist and Surrealist art and literature communities in London, but by the 1950s her focus shifted. Not only did she begin joining occult and magical organizations, but her investigations into witchcraft began in earnest, and she relocated permanently to the west of Cornwall. Her strictly magical essays proliferated and she also had success in publishing her spiritual and mystical travel guides, *Crying of the Wind* (1955) an experiential

Amy Hale

guide to Ireland, and also *The Living Stones* (1957), which is probably one of the first Earth Mysteries guides to Cornwall.

Colquhoun emerges as a nexus of all of the major occult currents of the 20th century. What follows is a very short resume of her esoteric interests: she was very firmly entrenched in the Western esoteric tradition, but was also well read in Asian traditions, including Buddhism and yoga. Kaballah and alchemy were probably the most consistent references throughout her body of work, followed by her interest in Druidry and nature religion. She was an initiate of a wide variety of different orders representing Hermetic and Pagan traditions, including the OTO (Typhonian and possibly Caliphate), Co-Masonry, British Circle of the Universal Bond, the Golden Section Society, and in later years the Fellowship of Isis. Although she was unsuccessful at her attempts to become an initiate of Mathers' Golden Dawn, the Golden Dawn system of magic was clearly one of her guiding principles, and she wrote the influential account of the Golden Dawn magicians, *The Sword of Wisdom*, published in 1975. She may have also been a key member of a Golden Dawn type organization The Ancient Order of the Phoenix, founded by Tamara Bourkhoun. She also worked briefly with Dion Fortune's group Society for Inner Light, but did not continue on with them. She had deep interests in and knowledge of both traditional and contemporary witchcraft, met with Gerald Gardner more than once, yet did not become a member of any Wiccan organization. Although she was not a spiritualist, she had knowledge of and correspondence with folk healers around Britain and Ireland, and made extensive use of remote healing services.

Despite Colquhoun's fortunes with various Hermetic organizations, it is very clear from studying her entire corpus of material that it was the Golden Dawn system which held the most interest for her and underpinned the symbolism of her work until a very late stage of her life. Color was a very important aspect of her work. She took a very precise interest in ensuring that the colors she used for invocations were correct, and she theorized about the magical use of color in a number of essays throughout her life. For her the Rose Cross was a very detailed color wheel, and in her notes and poems there were frequent references to color formulas and color mixing. The more perfect the colors, the more one could be assured of success in creating flashing tablets, visual invocations of angels, deities and intelligences, and of course tarot cards.

As early as the 1940s, Colquhoun started a number of artistic experiments called the Alchemical series. They seem to be a combination of automatic techniques, and highly controlled artistic invocations. She would start the process with color schemes drawn from either alchemical works, or from Golden Dawn texts. She frequently employed grids to her figure drawings, starting from the base and working up through the figure, using Kaballistic attributions and correspondences for the body and times of day. She would then overlay the designs with colors taken from particular schema. She describes grided images very similar to this in a section of her alchemical novel *Goose of Hermogenes*. She also worked quite frequently with cubes, and grids within the cubes, envisioning figures and temples within three dimensional and four dimensional spaces.

She also used color in capturing alchemical processes. As previously noted, the creation of the hermaphrodite was one of the most persistent themes in her art. Like a woman obsessed, she created numerous studies in watercolor of the hermaphrodite, using red and blue on a conjoined figure seen from the side. It frequently appeared as though the paint was applied using what would be considered an automatic technique, but in other instances the paint was more carefully applied, accompanying sketches of both human and angelic lovers. Red and blue also appear in her poetry as continuing themes indicating the hermaphrodite being generated through an alchemical process.

In 1977, she developed a pack of tarot cards. She had used tarot images previously as stand-alone works, but this was her own set of divinatory materials. They are pure color based on Golden Dawn systems of coloring, and in the accompanying essay she states that they were created using the psycho morphological technique of color placement used by other Surrealists. It is clear that Colquhoun believed in the power of color as sufficient communicators with otherworldly interlocutors. In her deck one does not require images to create stories, the colors alone provide the necessary psychic link, that will shape the narrative for the reader.

Colquhoun's 1961 surrealist novel *Goose of Hermogenes* is a very interesting example of the ways in which she combines Surrealist and esoteric art principles. The book seems to work on a number of levels and she is basically creating a narrative through highly coded alchemical tracts. It is loosely a story about a girl who has been lured by her uncle to his strange island, to help him in some way and his pursuit of the Philosopher's Stone. The book is replete with alchemical imagery, each chapter of the book representing a stage of alchemical processing. Much of the work is an amalgam of alchemical visual images set on paper. One of the chapters directs the narrative through the images of the 1625 Book of Lambspring by Nicholas Barnaud. Despite being challenging reading, *Goose of Hermogenes* works on several different levels, both as an automatic surrealist text, and also as a well constructed alchemical allegory.

Ithell and Paganism

Colquhoun was involved in several different organizations that eventually became what we would know as modern Paganism. Ithell believed that her Scottish ancestry predisposed her to the type of second sight and "Celtic sensitivity" that would make her Surrealism more successful. So in tandem with her Hermetic pursuits, Ithell also investigated witchcraft, Druidry, and other Celtic orders, culminating in her initiation into the Fellowship of Isis towards the end of her life. There is a persistent theme of the relationship between women and nature in her work long before there was anything like a cohesive or coherent Goddess movement. Her interest in Celtic spirituality focused on the land itself and of sacred sites, and also with the transmission of tradition embodied in a location.

In pursuing these interests, Ithell took initiations with and studied with a number of organizations, however, she had a common pattern of studying the curriculum earnestly, only to be frustrated by the lack of knowledge displayed by senior members of the order. She was frequently found to be difficult or argumentative, and too challenging in her questions on the curriculum. For instance in the 1960s she was a member of the Druidic order The Circle of the Universal Bond, also known as *An Druidh Uileach Braithrearchas*. Although she engaged in a very vigorous discussion about the Order's first level of work, she told officials she was not interested in taking initiation beyond that. She was an associate of Colin Murray from the 1950s, and a very supportive member of his Celtic-based Golden Section Order until very late in her life, being the most active in the 1970s.

Within Celtic spirituality, her interest in Druidry was probably the most significant to her work, but it was more of an influence on her poetry and her essay writing than on her visual work, which continued to be more significantly marked by her alchemical and hermetic symbolism. One could theorize that this is because of the emphasis on the Bard and divine revelation within

Celtic traditions, which would have been consistent with her Surrealist practice. As a result, there are many Celtic topics covered within Ithell's "found poems."

Her visual art demonstrated a belief in lay lines and Earth mysteries before such concepts became more prevalent in British alternative spirituality. Her 1942 oil painting "Dance of the Nine Opals" shows the Merry Maidens stone circle near Penzance, where each of the stones is revealed to be an opal, stone of Mercury and alchemical process. Each stone is linked in a geometric pattern of energy, fed from the ground, turning the site into a center of energy. Given that the belief in magnetic earth currents was not a widely accepted feature of British esoteric culture for over another two decades, this painting alone demonstrates the degree to which Colquhoun was ahead of her time in synthesizing diverse strands of occult belief.

Ithell Colquhoun was a remarkably prolific artist, deep and creative thinker and an uncompromising woman. Even a cursory glance at her artistic production shows that in her pursuit of the Great Work, she left few stones unturned and few systems unconsidered, and for this reason, exploring her vast creative output is challenging. Colquhoun's legacy is the story of a woman who was not afraid to challenge conventional thought about sexuality, and who reconsidered women's position and power in both an earthly and sacred sense. And of course, she is a fine example of how women do magic.

References

Ades, Dawn (1980). "Notes on Two Women Surrealist Painters: Eileen Agar and Ithell Colquhoun." *Oxford Art Journal 1980*, 36-43.

Ades, Dawn. "Surrealism, Male-Female." Mundy, Jennnifer (editor). *Surrealism, Desire Unbound*. London: Tate Publishing, 2001.

Chadwick, Whitney (1985). *Women Artists and the Surrealist Movement*. New York: Thames and Hudson.

Colquhoun, Ithell (1981). "Letter to the Editor." *Oxford Art Journal 1981*, 65.

Colquhoun, Ithell (1949). "The Mantic Stain" *Enquiry, Volume 2 Number 4*, 15-21.

Colquhoun, Ithell (1955). *The Crying of the Wind*. London: Peter Owen.

Colquhoun, Ithell (1961). *Goose of Hermogenes*. London: Peter Owen.

Colquhoun, Ithell (1957). *The Living Stones*. London: Peter Owen.
Colquhoun, Ithell (1975). *The Sword of Wisdom (1975)*. New York: GP Putnam.
Mundy, Jennifer, editor (2001). *Surreealism: Desire Unbound*. London: Tate Publishing.
Polizzotti, Mark (1995). *Revolution of the Mind: The Life of Andre Breton*. New York: Farar, Straus and Giroux.
Rosemont, Penelope (editor) (1998). *Surrealist Women: An International Anthology*. Austin: University of Texas Press.

Biography

Amy Hale is an anthropologist specializing in contemporary Celtic cultures, with an emphasis on modern Cornwall and British esoteric cultural history. She is the co-editor of *New Directions in Celtic Studies* (2000) and *Inside Merlin's Cave: A Cornish Arthurian Reader* (2000) in addition to over 30 other articles ranging from Neo-Druidry to Celtic cultural tourism. Her book, *Raising Piran's Standard: Cornish Identity Politics and Economic Policy*, is forthcoming from LIT Verlag in 2010. She is the co-editor of the *Journal of the Academic Study of Magic 5* and her biography on Ithell Colquhoun, *Brighter than Crystal*, is forthcoming from Francis Boutle Press (2010).

HERMETIC WOMEN

Although it comes as a surprise to many that women work the Ceremonial magical currents, contemporary women practice all of the magical arts. These women face the same challenges and tasks that many Western women undertake, to raise children, care for the sick and elderly, maintain a household and a job, while fitting a magical practice in around the demands of daily life.

Here Lesa Whyte breaks new ground in her discussion of a pregnant magician's approach to magic. Soror Inde Seraphina surveys the change in her Enochian practice since the birth of her daughter; Shellay Maughan combs through abramelin oil recipes while meditating on what really matters; and Kayla Block reaches a new understanding of talismanic magic while working for a dying friend. Helen Honeycutt views alchemy through a feminist lens, and Kat Sanborn picks her way through a stiff childhood to her magical path. All sift through what they do to find the essence of what will work in the context of their lives.

MAGIC AND PREGNANCY
LESA WHYTE

"The Man delights in uniting with the Woman; the Woman in parting from the Child."

Aleister Crowley, Book of Lies (15)

When I was pregnant with my second child, I had been actively involved in the Western Magical Tradition for a number of years. I was familiar with the symbolism of pregnancy being useful in contemplating certain principles, such as the idea of potential as it pertains to the cycle of life and death. Something with which I was not familiar, however, was how the process of pregnancy and childbirth would affect my work as a magical practitioner. Would I need to stop all magical work? Would changing my practices be sufficient? Why would I need to stop or change my practices in the first place? What are the ethical issues involved with performing theurgic magic (that is, magic that acts on one's Self rather than on the world external to Self)? How would the flow of energy shift now that I was carrying another being inside of my body?

What about the fact that now, within my body, were two sets of energy points? Two "middle pillars?" (Head, throat, heart, etc.)

Naturally, I asked all of my magical acquaintances and friends for assistance. I developed a sort of informal survey:

1. Has anything been written regarding the practice of magic by a pregnant woman?

2. Has anything been written about the physical state of pregnancy from a magical perspective?

3. What kinds of practices are permitted for pregnant women by various magical schools and fraternal organizations?

4. What kinds of practices could be adapted for use by a pregnant woman?

And finally,

5. What is the relationship between magic and pregnancy?

Although these questions may sound similar on first inspection, there are some nuances that give them distinction. For example, we may view the state of pregnancy from a magical perspective that will allow it to be used successfully as a symbol. And while there may be several practices that could be adapted with moderate effort to be used appropriately by a pregnant woman, there is a vast difference between that situation and having material actually written FOR a pregnant woman. Finally, the relationship between magic and pregnancy transcends questions of usefulness in symbolism and praxis to the very existence of a model in the Western Magical Tradition that applies to women in this state.

I began this search with the rather naive belief that something *must* have been written for a pregnant practitioner. After all, Hermetic magic has been practiced by women for at least 100 years; this we know. Unfortunately, we have no numbers on how many may have been practicing during that time, and it is generally assumed that women have been a small minority. If we suppose a small number of women practicing at a given time and subtract those who became pregnant at some point during their active practice of magic, I estimate that the number will become very small indeed. This is not to say that woman magical practitioners have not been concerned about doing magic during pregnancy, only that if they have, precious little has been written about it.

It is my hope that by writing this piece, I will provide at least a starting place for women who are active in the Western Magical Tradition to begin their own remarkable journey of discovery during pregnancy. The magic that we learn and practice during our usual state of existence doesn't necessarily apply to our pregnant state, and it is such a little-explored area that we will have ample opportunity to develop insights never made or recorded. I consider this situation to be a major blind spot in the eye of the Western Magical Tradition, and as magical practitioners, you and I have the awesome responsibility of blazing new inroads for the women who will come after us.

Lesa Whyte

The Great Initiation

Pregnancy, regardless of its path or outcome, is an initiation. Anthropologists have done a remarkable job of defining the typical elements of initiation rituals and rites of passage ceremonies done throughout the world, and almost without fail, they include these components:

1. Death to the old state of being
2. A liminal state during which transformation occurs
3. Introduction to the world in the initiate's new state of existence

I was astounded when I came across this model. At first glance, I thought to myself that pregnancy followed these steps exactly. But upon further examination, it occurred to me that pregnancy has been occurring in our species far longer than rites of passage. Is it possible, or even likely, that the model of initiation itself is based upon the process of pregnancy and childbirth, and not the other way around?

Initiation	Pregnancy
1. Death to old state of being	1. Pregnancy
2. Liminal state; transition	2. Childbirth, until the moment the child emerges
3. New state of existence	3. New life with child; new identity as mother

I'd like to explore each of these states a bit more.

STEP 1: Pregnancy; Death to the Old

In discussing pregnancy and magic, there will necessarily be much said on the subject of death. In this case, however, death is used as a metaphor. Upon the moment of conception, that very moment when the father's sperm cell penetrates the mother's ovum, the mother's body begins to symbolically "die" to its former state. Before the mother even knows she is pregnant, changes begin taking place that will separate her from the physical realities known by a non-pregnant woman. At first, these changes are purely physical, then later, mental and emotional. Little by little, over the space of 283 days, the woman is literally a creature apart; she is not male, and she is not a typical female. She is a female who carries within her the beginnings of another human life.

The 9 months of pregnancy represent the mother's "death" to her previous, unpregnant self. Her habits may change, her ways of thinking may change, and her physical appearance certainly changes. All of these things serve to remind her that she is not who she was before.

STEP 2: Childbirth; the Liminal State

A liminal state is an "in-between" state. For example, twilight and dawn, existing between full light and full darkness, are liminal states. Liminality is a state of ambiguity and lack of definition, the "betwixt and between." In a magical initiation, this state is sometimes represented by the initiate being stripped of any earlier signs of self without yet having had a new identity conferred upon him or her. It is a state of chaos from which one emerges into a newly organized existence.

I am tempted to say that this stage of an initiation is the *most* magical, but in actuality, it wouldn't be nearly as remarkable if the first stage hadn't already taken place. Certainly it would still be an adventure, an "ordeal" of the highest order through which anyone would emerge a changed person, but spending time in advance of this stage experiencing life as someone other than your usual self does have a preparatory affect. By the time this stage arrives, the initiate is ready; often they are very frightened, but they realize that they have reached the point of no return. All that remains for them to do is cross the narrow bridge between worlds.

Childbirth has long been connected to the myths of travel to the underworld. As an example of why this would be the case, recall the story of Innana, who visits the underworld to see her sister, Ereshkigal, the Queen of the Great Earth. Innana enters the underworld as the Queen of Heaven, wearing her usual badges and symbols of royalty and goddess-hood. However, as she descends, she is made to relinquish an item at each level of the underworld until she finally reaches the bottom, completely nude and vulnerable. There, she goes through an ordeal where she is hung on a hook for three days before she is able to again ascend into the light.

In childbirth, women often enter the experience with many preconceived notions of how they will perform, what it will be like, how the entire experience will play out. Often her first stage of labor goes uneventfully; some contractions that are tolerable are perhaps the only signal that she is about to enter a liminal state. As labor progresses, however, she finds herself descending further and further into herself, into her body and into the experience, which often bears no resemblance to her original notions of what it would be like. This is very much like Innana being forced to give up her symbols of royalty and beauty; a woman in labor gives up her intellectual connection to what labor *should* be like until she eventually accepts what it *is*. While she may have many birth attendants supporting her during this process, there comes a point where it is the birthing woman alone within herself, naked, vulnerable, at the point where she is taken over by the process and her body. And thus her ordeal is sustained until the final breaking point where the child emerges from her body and is at last separated into its own existence apart from her.

STEP 3: Motherhood; Re-introduction to the World

In a magical initiation ritual, the initiate often receives a new name by which he will be known in his future work with his initiators. In a wedding ceremony, the couple is re-introduced to the congregation by their new, joint identity. The new name that a woman receives after giving birth is "mother."

After the child is separated from the mother's body, there begins a period of time often referred to as "the fourth trimester." It is during this period of time that a woman adjusts to her new identity as her child's mother, and to her new body which is neither pregnant nor the same as her pre-pregnant body. Things will never be quite the same in the woman's life. This is not to say that they will not be *good*, only that they will be *different*. It is entirely up to the woman after the passage of time to make judgments on how to value her life as a mother versus her life before children.

In cultures that have a very strong social structure, the new mother is rarely left alone to deal with her new existence; in Western culture, a woman is often expected to be "back to normal" in no time at all. Only recently has there been an acknowledgement that post-partum mothers need strong social and community support. As with initiation and rite of passage rituals, the newly-emerged initiate needs to be shown acceptance and encouragement as they learn to function in their new role.

Where You Put Your Energy

One of the main points that were discussed when I began asking questions about this topic was related to how a woman directs her energy during pregnancy. There seemed to be a consensus that when a practitioner is pregnant, she should be directing all of her energy to the health of her child, not toward enlightenment or any other magical goal. Some magicians are very attached to this point, but very few gave actual reasons for this belief, and I was amazed by some of the dire warnings that came along as justifications. One magician in particular swore that he has known women who practice magic during pregnancy and all of them have had problems ranging from difficult labors to diseased children, to death. As scary as all of this might sound, he gave not one logical, magical reason why this would be the case.

The fact is that, upon deep reflection, I happened upon some very good reasons for not practicing magic that will interfere with the flow of energy from you to your child. Fortunately, they have very little to do with the kinds of superstitious "do it and you'll die / go crazy / have a deformed baby" warnings that I was given.

The Goals of Theurgy

In the Western Magical Tradition, one of the primary goals of magic that works on the Self is to achieve a connection to the part of one's Self that is in contact with the Divine. This is an intentionally vague description because the ways that different schools of magical thought teach on this point often use different language. I have been trained in a Golden Dawn-style tradition, so the language that I am familiar with is that of the Holy Guardian Angel. In essence, the practitioner does his or her work to ascend toward something called Knowledge and Conversation with their Holy Guardian Angel, at which point he or she becomes an Adept and will then be led in future magical workings through the wisdom of this connection.

We may shorten the above description by saying that the primary goal of magic until Adepthood is that of achieving union. Consider that the symbolism most often associated with the striving toward Knowledge and Conversation is that of marital union (i.e., sex), and you immediately have some idea of the working. Two beings, whether conceived as internal or external in origin, are trying to come together. We may visualize this process in the following way:

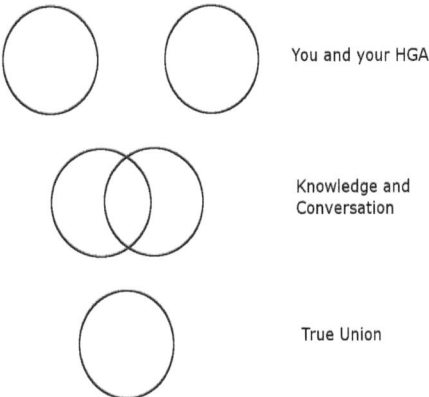

Now, take the process of pregnancy from a similar perspective. Your work during pregnancy is to grow your baby inside of your body with the end goal being that of separation. The baby develops so that eventually, it may exist outside of your body. We can visualize this process thus:

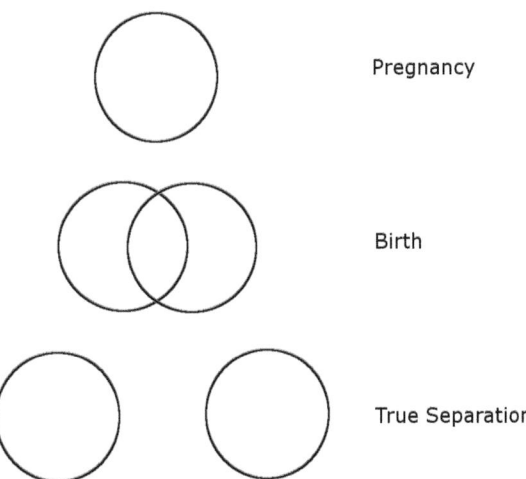

Magic and Pregnancy

As you can see through a symbolic representation of these two processes, they are diametrically opposed. Perhaps one *could* set out to achieve union and separation at the same time, but my magical training tells me that there would be some serious confusion on the etheric level about which energies should be going in which direction. Perhaps *this* could cause unpleasant manifestations in the physical world, such as sickness and disease, but I believe that the magical implications alone are enough to warrant an advisory to not practice both at once, whether pregnant or not.

Does this mean that a pregnant woman should not practice magic? No, I don't believe it does. It means that the pregnant practitioner must be cognizant of the processes that are in play during this time, and work within them to achieve the best possible results. Pregnancy is not the time to perform the Abramelin Operation, for example, a six month retirement during which the practitioner focuses all of his or her energy on achieving Knowledge and Conversation with the Holy Guardian Angel. Pregnancy is not the time to start summoning spirits, a practice which requires the utmost discipline of will and a very stable energetic reserve. Pregnancy is the time that nature has given women to focus on growing their babies to be healthy, and to learn about the process of separation. This can be a profoundly magical undertaking, and a very important one at that.

The Vesica Piscis

In the models of separation and union above, the shape of the vesica piscis is important in understanding the dynamic movement of energy.

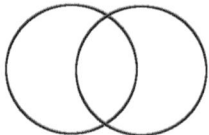

In recent years, the vesica piscis has been tossed around casually as a symbol of the Feminine Divine, and therefore of the Womb. It is quite unfortunate that the Western Magical Tradition has utterly confused kteic (vaginal) symbolism with womb symbolism. The vesica piscis is clearly a kteic symbol, representing the passage to and from the womb. Look at the two models above; you will see that the vesica piscis is present during the active phase of union and separation. If the womb is a noun, the vesica piscis would be a verb. It is a passage, a path, a method, a means to an end. On one end of this passage there is union, on the other side, separation.

Physically, the vesica piscis represents the process by which a child is created, that is, through the act of sexual intercourse. The vagina is the female feature which facilitates this *process*. It is the passage through which the male may deliver his sperm to the woman's ovum, which is awaiting fertilization. The flip side of this situation is, of course, pregnancy and childbirth. During childbirth the vagina is known as "the birth canal;" it is the *passage* by which the baby descends from the mother's womb into the outside world.

Magically, this is a very important distinction. To say that the vesica piscis represents the womb is like saying that the phallus represents the testes. They are clearly different pieces of physiology, and are clearly different principles.

The Cabala

As a Hermeticist, I've become quite fond of working with Cabalistic material, and using the Tree of Life as a model for understanding the dynamic interplay of energies. It came as a surprise to me though (and perhaps it shouldn't have) that in spite of inspiring a great deal of material dealing with symbols of sexuality, fertility, birth and death, there was no Cabalistic material I could find dealing directly with the state of pregnancy.

What follows is an analysis of four points on the Tree of Life that are particularly relevant to a pregnant magical practitioner. I must add here that if one wishes to extend this analysis to a state of symbolic or spiritual pregnancy, these associations could be used to gain more insight into such a perspective.

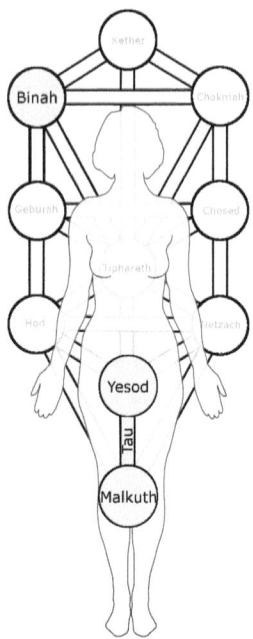

Diagram 4 shows the female human body with the Tree of Life mapped onto it. Most diagrams of this sort show either a male or androgynous figure, presumably because most magical and Cabalistic practitioners in the past have been male. As a female practitioner, I believe it's high time we women begin reinterpreting the material of the Western Magical Tradition through our own eyes and experience. This impulse, however, could fill a volume of its own and is beyond the scope of this article.

If you follow the Path of Creation down the Tree, Binah accepts the energy of Kether and Chokmah. The energy now flows down the Tree, picking up the crucial elements necessary to do nothing short of *create*. In Yesod, the object of creation is finalized and grown into its ultimate state before descending through Tau into Malkuth. Often, those of us practicing in the Western magical tradition are so concerned with the Path of Return that we fail to give attention to the manifestation of creation all around us, every day. Hermeticism can be a highly intellectual, masculine, solar tradition, and its attendant allegories often lofty and complex. The Path of Creation, however, is beautifully and powerfully illustrated by what has been called the most ordinary miracle in the world: the process of pregnancy and childbirth.

Binah

Binah is the third sphere on the Tree of Life. It is at the head of what has been called both the Pillar of Form and the Pillar of Severity. The name Binah means "understanding" and nicknames for this sphere are Marah (the great sea), Aima (the great fertile mother) and Ama (the great sterile mother). The color most often associated with Binah is black. We can picture Binah as a great black ocean that holds the potential for life and death.

On the surface, this conjures up images of dark goddesses, but in actuality, it is Binah's life-giving capacity that holds the secrets of these images. Dion Fortune, in her book "The Mystical Qabalah," explained that Binah accepts the energy directed from Kether and sent out by Chokmah, and then begins the process by which this creative energy will be given form. Binah is the primordial mother; she takes the abstract and gives it order. By giving birth, she bestows mortality, which gives death. The organization of energy into the polarities of life and death are both present in Binah, which is why it sits atop the Pillar of Severity. Binah, in essence, starts to shape The Light into a form that will be conducive to manifestation in the less subtle worlds approaching the physical.

Binah's planetary association is Saturn. Often, Saturn is given what seem to be very masculine attributes, but when you consider them in association with Binah, you can view them in a feminine light. The marking of time, for example, is very closely associated with Binah because it is in this sphere that organization of the abstract takes place.

Yesod

Yesod is the "Foundation." Given that a foundation is an underpinning, let's look at this sphere as the foundation of creation: the means by which a creative impulse is manifested in the physical world. How is that accomplished by humanity? Quite often, by procreation. The traditional physical attribution of this sphere, "the reproductive organs" or "the genital region" is, unfortunately, woefully inadequate. As I've commented above that "womb" has been confused with kteic symbolism, Yesod is the sphere most frequently saddled with this confusion.

Translated into specific female physiology, I prefer to associate Yesod with the ovaries and uterus, the organs by which a creative impulse from the father and the mother grows into physical existence. This is not the passage of the creative impulse into the physical world; this is where the energies and dynamics of the upper spheres are condensed into their final form before manifesting in this world.

The Path of Tau

Malkuth is the 32nd and final path in the process of creation.

An interesting attribute of Tau is that it shares a Saturn association with Binah, which link the two closely. Like Binah, Tau is accepting the issue of the spheres above and is delivering it into manifestation in Malkuth. It is finishing the task that Binah has begun.

The vesica piscis, mentioned earlier, is the critical door through which we can understand existence as a two-way interplay of energy. The Path of Return (the Serpent's Path) flows from Malkuth along the Path of Tau, through Yesod and then onward up the tree. The Path of Creation (the Lightning Flash) flows down the Tree, finally being realized in Malkuth after descending the Path of Tau. We can establish associations between the Path of Tau, the vesica piscis, and female kteic imagery. Tau facilitates sexual union and birth, depending on the direction of energies.

Because it is the last one traversed before manifestation in the physical world, and is the first traversed on the Path of Return, Tau is an enigmatic path. Images associated with Tau are descent into the underworld, caverns, underground rivers, danger and life-threatening challenges. A journey through Tau is like one of the Tasks of Hercules; it is a non-trivial trial that one must pass in order to progress.

The path of Tau is the point on the Tree of Life which holds the most critical lessons for a pregnant magical practitioner. In the process of childbirth as an initiation, Tau represents the second, liminal stage during which the woman must go within herself, travel the narrow bridge between worlds, and separate the child from her body. In Africa, there is a tribe in which a pregnant woman who begins labor will tell her older children, "I am going away to the sea to get our new child. But the sea is a very dangerous place, and I might not return." Like the journey of Inanna into the underworld, traveling the Path of Tau can be a dangerous proposition.

Malkuth

The final sphere is, of course, Malkuth, "Kingdom," the world of physical manifestation. It is here that we get to see with our human eyes what creation hath wrought. Malkuth is associated with the Earth, with the tangible, with the final culmination of activities taking place on higher levels of existence. Malkuth, in effect, is at the bottom of a cosmic "trickle-down" effect.

The child borne of its mother exists in Malkuth. The mother has undergone the trial of her life, perhaps enduring significant danger or injury, to bring a new creation into existence. She has completed the process of separation; she has nurtured the flow of energies from beginning to end. The results, as we all know with matters of life and childbirth, are unpredictable; like any initiation, the results are sometimes happy, sometimes sad. The fact remains, however, that whatever the outcome, the woman who emerges on the other side of this powerful initiation is not the same woman who stood at the beginning.

Magical Practice During Pregnancy

And so, after performing my own investigation, my answer to the question "should a pregnant woman practice magic?" is "it all depends." There *are*, as it turns out, some compelling reasons that I've been given for a woman to not practice theurgic magic during pregnancy, including:

* A woman has been given 9 months to focus her energy on growing the baby within her, that's what she should do.
* A woman who practices magic in an unskilled manner opens herself and her child to the effects of imbalance. This would include the potential misdirection of specific types of energies.
* The child is a conscious entity and therefore should have some say in any magic that is performed on its body.

Above all I recommend relying upon your own understanding and illumination rather than relying on the opinions of men, or women who have never been pregnant. I would, and have, erred on the side of caution by limiting my own practice while sorting through these questions, and would recommend any other pregnant magical practitioner to do the same. Be moderate. Be careful. Be considerate of the child within you. It seems no more ethical to perform experimental magic on your fetus than on a child already existing outside of your body.

Timing

If you do decide to practice magic, particularly theurgic, during your pregnancy, the matter of "when" is one that should be considered. The philosopher Aristotle wrote in his "The History of Animals" that a fetus can be considered "ensouled" at 40 to 90 days after conception, depending on when and where fetal movement is first detected. The debate about the soul and viability of a fetal life is beyond the scope of this article, so I leave it to the reader to determine for herself at what point their unborn child is an entity unto itself, capable of generating and receiving spiritual energies. This is, I believe, a critical question to ask oneself before any magical undertaking during pregnancy.

Divination

One magician I spoke to during my research suggested that some kind of scrying work to make contact with the unborn child might be called for, to simply ask permission before doing energy work. As magical practitioners we make contact with a variety of energies on other levels of existence as a matter of course. Shouldn't it go without saying that we should ask our own children, part of us but other, if it's permissible to move energy around while they're busy trying to grow?

Many mothers experience a strong connection with their unborn children spontaneously, sometimes through dreams or intuition. We should not rule out visionary work as appropriate during pregnancy when the goal is something that often occurs naturally. This could be accomplished through methods such as scrying, tarot, meditation, dreamwork, or other modes of divination.

Conclusion

Early in my pregnancy, before researching the topic discussed in this article, I was practicing some very basic ritual work including the Middle Pillar. (If you aren't familiar with the Middle Pillar, it involves calling down light into one's body, focusing it in the centers of the body along the Middle Pillar, and circulating it within and without.) At some point around the time when my baby's heart started beating approximately 10 weeks in gestation, I experienced a severe reaction to the ritual; my own heart began to race, I felt dizzy and sensed dread. Usually these are symptoms consistent with a panic attack, something I'd never experienced before or since. I stopped practicing for the time and then devoted my attention to the research presented here. It is possible the reaction was due to anxiety about the effects of magic on my child, or perhaps because my child and my body were unaccustomed to the ritual in this state. Whatever the case, there was a new element in this working that I'd not experienced before, and it needed to be examined. Eventually I reintroduced light energy work, mostly in the form of gentle meditations where I incorporated my unborn child as a party to my own prayers to the Divine.

There are a couple of points I would like to share in conclusion regarding the types of workings that seem appropriate and not appropriate to me, after carefully examining the possibilities.

One thing I definitely would rule out is summoning work or work that involves taking on an angelic entity or god-form. A pregnant woman is already hosting another being; inviting another one into their body seems like a recipe for unpredictable results. Not doing *goetic* summoning, I believe, should go without saying. These are things that seem like common sense *to me*, but as I learned from my informal survey, there is no clear consensus. However, given the reaction I experienced to a beneficial ritual such as the Middle Pillar, I personally would never invite any outside intelligence into a body occupied by my child.

This brings us back to the work of union with the Holy Guardian Angel. Should it be done during pregnancy? Isn't it intended to be the Work of Light, for the benefit of ourselves and the world? It's entirely possible that a pregnant woman could do HGA work all through her pregnancy with marvelous results. Years after the birth of my child, I've continued to devote thought to this, however, and have decided to recommend against it. To accomplish

Knowledge and Conversation with one's Holy Guardian Angel, one must work an operation of UNION. To accomplish the birth of a child, one must work an operation of SEPARATION. Even the most experienced magical practitioners sometimes have difficulty maintaining the strength, discipline and focus needed to accomplish their workings, particularly those performed at the level of an adept. I, personally, would not want to focus separation energy on my HGA or union energy on my unborn child.

When you are one in your body, you may decide for yourself. However, when your body is a refuge and temple for another, you must maintain it with the utmost sanctity and preservation. You must focus on the initiation through which you are now traveling, and devote yourself to it in order to reap the benefits and lessons. If done properly, I believe wholeheartedly that a pregnancy can be a deeply meaningful, mystical and magical experience.

As in all things, as above, so below.

References

Fortune, Dion (1987). *The Mystical Qabbalah*. Wellingborough, Northamptonshire: Aquarian Press.

Biography

Lesa Whyte has been exploring matters of Hermetic spirituality since 1994. She has co-founded and studied in magical lodges in Seattle, led Hermetic study groups, performed extensive individual work and written several online articles on topics ranging from the history of magic to the Art of Memory. Her dedicated focus for many years has been on researching the figure of Mary Magdalene, on whom she has presented a Hermetic perspective through talks at the Seattle Pagan Scholars, the Theosophical Society, and a 1999 article in SageWoman Magazine. Her book *The Complete Idiot's Guide to Mary Magdalene* (Alpha) was published in 2004 under her married name. In 2006 she contributed material to the anthology, "The Secrets of Mary Magdalene" (Vanguard Press), and was featured in the associated DVD. Lesa lives with her family in the Seattle area where she and her husband collect books on magic, folklore, and religion.

ENOCHIAN MOTHERHOOD
SOROR INDE SERAPHINA

I'm looking at my notebook with many "trip reports" from scrying the Enochian Aethyrs, most of them from the time before I became pregnant with my daughter. For me, the process of scrying the aethyrs is an amazing and important spiritual process to know the Divine and each experience in the aethyrs opens the way more and more for that relationship to grow. I wanted to continue the work after my daughter was born, although I knew it is easy in the pressure of learning to care for a newborn (then infant, then toddler, etc.) to "never have time" to do certain kinds of magical work. The purpose of this essay is to share how I learned to compress the time needed for certain magical work to fit the schedule of a new mama.

Scrying the Aethyrs: Before Baby

Before my daughter was born, I had a great deal of free time to devote to magical work. I would create a ritual bath, with aromatherapy related to the aethyr if I had already been in it and knew what the themes were. I always wore ritual garments and jewelry. Although one aethyr clearly called for my full English Traditional witchcraft regalia, usually I would wear a white robe/dress with something red (tabard/stole/scarf). To open the temple, I would light candles, burn incense, use Abremelin oil, put up Enochian tablets, etc. I would always use the same incense each time. For the first year or so, I used a homemade frankincense/myrrh/sandalwood mix on charcoal, but then went to "pearls" of frankincense exclusively because it creates less particulate. Indoor air quality can actually be a problem for many magicians – but that is another essay.

Then I would ground and center and perform the Lesser Banishing Ritual of the Pentagram (LBRP). Some of my fellow aethyrists use the Hexagram ritual here, but didn't feel it added much for me. And then I would cast a simple Wiccan (Georgian) circle. This confuses some people, but basically I like to be "inside" a cast circle when I am going to leave and go exploring. Others do not do this because they don't feel they need it and it seems to be just fine. Then I would perform the Supreme/Greater Invoking

Pentagram Ritual (SIRP) to charge the tablets or at least invoke the elements (again). (I actually found that having the tablets out or not, charged or not, did not change the results of the aethyr scrying for me.)

    Then, I would recite my personal prayer to my Holy Guardian Angel (HGA) written in Enochian. This is a short heartfelt prayer of devotion and thanks for the opportunity to do this work and also asking for the Angel's protection and guidance. Then I would recite the 18th Call, mostly because I think it is really beautiful and to me it is one that most helps me express my gratitude that I have an opportunity to do this work. Sometimes I would omit this and it didn't seem to make a difference in the results. Finally, I would recite the 19th Call and insert the name of the aethyr I am working with. I usually used a format where I could see the Enochian letterforms, the Enochian words and the English translation all at the same time. I don't think it really matters for the results – I just like to know what I am saying in a foreign language. Then I vibrated the Aethyr Governors' names. Sometimes I did this before I did the 19th call. It worked either way. Then a meditation/trance period which varied greatly in length, but usually not more than a half hour to 45 minutes. Then I would write and draw extensively in my Aethyr journal. To close, I would do a prayer to HGA and thanks to the Governors. I would perform a LBRP and occasionally go through the banishing version of the Greater Pentagram Ritual. I would take down the formal Georgian circle, close the temple and do any needed grounding.

    Total time: approximately one to two hours.

Scrying the Aethyrs: After Baby

This section could have been called: "Is it possible to remove most of the "ceremonial" from the magic and still have an effective learning experience in the Enochian Aethyrs during the space of the average toddler nap"? Answer: Yes.

    While the temple set up has greatly changed in my current practice, the experience of working inside the aethyrs remains the same. (However, as Soror Kineta pointed out, maybe if I didn't already have so years of working this system I might not be able to cut this many corners and still have an effective scrying experience.)

    I began by building a book to help me organize the bare necessities needed to scry the Enochian aethyrs. I had planned to start over from the beginning (TEX) as recommended by Demian

Murphy, one of the best aethyrists and teachers I have encountered. I found a 6" x 6" 3-ring binder made of chipboard filled with chipboard pages that could be removed. I printed and pasted the elemental tablets, the tablet of union, a list of the aethyrs with their governors and the necessary Enochian calls and my personal prayer to my HGA. It is possible the tablets could be done away with too, but since I have already made them, it is easy to pop them out of the binder and use them.

I have only done this a few times and it is like the beginning of Mission Impossible. From the moment my daughter falls asleep, the fuse is lit and the theme music begins. I light a candle for my Angel (which has a wonderful scent), open the three-ring binder and pull out my new tablets (printed and pasted onto chipboard, no other work with them) and distribute them around me. Pull out other chipboards with names of aethyrs and their governors, the 18th and 19th calls and my special prayer to my HGA in Enochian. I do a superfast astral LBRP, visualize a cast circle, recite the Angel invocation at top speed, whisper the 18th call, whisper the 19th call and governors' names. Chant ODO CICLE QAA to myself and open in TEX or the aethyr to be scryed. Remind all parties we have very little time and we need to get right to work. At the end of the session (even if it ends abruptly), thank angels and governors. Blow out candle and put away. Put chipboards back in binder & instabanish. Total time: 45 minutes to open, scry, write notes, close and put everything away. Since my daughter's naps are between 45-60 minutes currently, it works!

What I find is that I am able to get in to the aethyrs as usual. (This in and of itself is great because I found I could not get into the aethyrs at all as soon as I became pregnant.) The first time I did this method, instead of starting over as planned in the most outer aethyr (TEX), I was directed (firmly) by the governors of TEX to BAG (into a new area I had not seen before) and then was "chutes and laddered" to a non-sequential aethyr, TOR, where I got my assignment and homework.

Subsequent visits using this method have also worked very well and in fact, just as well as the more elaborate set up from before my daughter's birth. My current tablets are not enhanced in any way and in fact, I didn't even activate them by doing the SIRP. I chanted (to myself) governor names appropriate for any "new" aethyrs as I entered them. It was nice to have the whole aethyr chart at hand since I didn't expect to be ushered to aethyrs I wasn't planning to call! My familiarity with the aethyrs I have already scryed was very useful because I knew where I was at all times and I knew TOR on sight.

"Skipping" aethyrs is highly unusual in my experience and is probably a factor of so much time spent in each aethyr in my past work and perhaps because I suggested in the set up that I wanted to get into the Work right away. I wouldn't want to skip any aethyr in which I had immediate work or any aethyr I hadn't already visited. In general, it was a successful experiment to hack the elaborate process I had been using and I may try to further compress the time needed to scry effectively.

What Are the Aethyrs anyway?

Based on the Enochian magical system of John Dee as interpreted by the Golden Dawn, the Enochian Aethyrs are visualized as a set of concentric circles in which the magician begins in the outermost aethyr (TEX) and proceeds inwards to the innermost aethyr (LIL). I was lucky to learn how to scry the Enochian Aethyrs from Jon Sewell, an excellent teacher of the system. Then Demian Murphy collaborated and compared notes with me and others he taught. Demian came up with the idea that while we might have somewhat common experiences in the "outer" aethyrs, we tend to see the emergence of a "personal qabala" that is unique to each person as the magician continues inwards in the aethyrs. Jon Sewell developed a related analogy that the aethyrs are like concentric circles of stained glass. As we get closer to the center, the stained glass is removed pane by pane and becomes ever more beautiful and illuminating.

In one of his aethyr visions, Jon saw that the aethyrs' content is supplied by the content of our souls, and that the light grew brighter as we approached the innermost aethyr, because the process was purifying. If the light is supplied by our individual souls, the "personal qabala" makes sense because the divine and our higher self will use the themes and images that resonate with us most deeply. Demian also proposed that the aethyrs seem to reveal the key elements of the particular point of view of the person going through them, unveiling more and more primary elements from which the consciousness of the person is composed. He describes that each person is a unique sort of knot, and each aethyr represents a step in the unraveling of that knot. Drawing on these descriptions, I would agree with the gravitational pull toward the center, which I would identify as the Divine and which others define as appropriate for themselves. I also think the aethyrs represent more and more challenging levels of personal and magical work which must be mastered before the next aethyr fully opens so that when the center levels are achieved, the person scrying them is prepared for what they represent.

General Thoughts on Aethyr Scrying

Several things about scrying the aethyrs have not changed for me regardless of how my temple is set up or how long that process takes. I always take my HGA and archangels with me, sort of like an "away team" on Star Trek. When I enter the aethyr, I make sure they are around me. I have never had to banish or otherwise confront anything sinister in the aethyrs (so far) but it is good to test and be cautious, as you would in any scrying. Which is not to say the aethyrs are not confrontational and challenging -- the aethyrs remind me of an initiation where you trust your initiators will guide you through the experience. It doesn't make it easier, but you know you are in safe hands.

It is pretty common in my experience with aethyrs that I am clearly *shown* the door/way/road/entry into the next aethyr when I am "done" with the current aethyr. My experience is that I am given assignments or homework that take a while to complete before I can move on to the next aethyr. Other people get different types of homework or no assignments at all. Some people complete all the aethyrs from TEX to LIL quickly and others take much longer and have repeated trips into each aethyr. I would stay in an aethyr (meaning I would return over and over) until the governors or angels showed me the door, literally. And I always got lots of homework, which I tended to complete before going back. That is, until I was directed to do homework *while* continuing the aethyr work and to return more often. It seemed the work needed to be started but not necessarily completed. Which is good, because some work may take years to complete!

I have heard enough of other's experiences in TEX to wish to provide some guidance for the first Aethyr one would scry. The first aethyr seems to be unique in that it is composed of 4 distinct quadrants (and possibly also a "center".) There are things to experience in each of the quadrants and it is very common to take multiple trips to TEX to experience each area. After that, each aethyr further "in" becomes more and more personal in the symbols used. While it is helpful to find a group of other people scrying the aethyrs and compare notes, I do suggest *not* reading accounts of the aethyr experiences of others or even the "titles" of aethyrs or what the aethyrs supposedly "mean," until you have done them on your own. And even then, keep in mind that the aethyrs are very personal and another magician's aethyr experiences will probably be unlike your own, especially as you proceed inwards.

I think it is very important to "keep your file cabinet full" by following your instincts or assignments and reading books, looking at or making art, travelling, etc. The aethyrs need to riffle through your brain to find stories, settings, images and symbols to communicate with you. The more that is handy in there, the more they (or your HGA) have to draw on, and the more useful the scrying experience will be. "Assignments" also tend to have the dual purpose of filling the filing cabinet for current or future aethyrs.

I had done a lot of Tree of Life pathworking and scrying before doing the aethyrs, and to me, the aethyrs felt decidedly "alien" -- not astral, not Tree, but something very different. Over time, the aethyrs feel much less strange, but one aethyr did take me to the Tree and I could tell right away I was in the Tree, not an aethyr. While I have seen systems linking the Aethyrs to paths on the Tree, I think such linkages are unique to each person and not really universal to the aethyrs based on comparisons of aethyr notes with other magicians.

Necessity is the Mother of Invention

In one phase of my life, I had abundant free time to scry the aethyrs. Currently, I am choosing to devote very little time to aethyr scrying. Right now, I love investing my time with my daughter and I trust that as she gets older, I will have more time for my personal and magical interests. As a result of my experiments, I would encourage women magicians who are feeling pressed for time because they are deeply engaged in educational, professional, artistic, family or other pursuits to experiment with how much magical infrastructure they need to get to the work. And then please write an essay about it, so we can continue to learn from each other as women and magicians.

Biography

Inde Seraphina is an operative magician, wiccan (Georgian line) and artist living in the Seattle area with her husband and young

Inde Seraphina

daughter. Two decades of varied magical study and exploration have led her to a primary practice of Enochian magic, particularly scrying the Enochian Aethyrs. She is an active member of the Open Source Order of the Golden Dawn-inspired Temple of Light and Darkness.

ARE INGREDIENTS IMPORTANT?
SHELLAY MAUGHAN

Today I'm making Abramelin oil. In preparation, I've read source materials, translations of source material, commentaries on the translations of the source material, and a variety of opinions on all of the above. I've spent weeks researching ingredients and where to buy them. I've learned about the different places cinnamon grows, what cassia is and what cassia isn't, the grades of myrrh and controversies surrounding myrrh, the toxicity (or lack of toxicity) of calamus. I've considered the astrological correspondences, symbolism, and mythologies of each ingredient. I've spent no small amount of money and a good chunk of my free time, but I'm satisfied that I have what I need.

It's a waxing moon, and it's a Sunday, and it's near but after Beltane. I'm ready. I carefully measure the ingredients, making sure the proportions are correct, seal the jar, and put it in a warm dark place. Over the next six weeks the properties of my ingredients will reveal themselves and merge together, guided by my intention, fueled by my Will, and pulled by the power of the Sun as it increases towards Midsummer. I am creating a magical tool of great potency.

That's one way of looking at it. Or I could say this: Using a recipe anybody could find online, I put some spices in a jar with olive oil and stuck it in the cupboard – after a few weeks the essential oils will combine and I'll have a nice perfume with an interesting history.

Sounds like two totally different activities, but they're exactly the same thing. It's all in how you look at it. And that's one of the most interesting questions in tradition-based magick; how we look at the tools we use in our rituals. Specifically, do the ingredients matter? How much? Why?

So, let's go back to Abramelin oil. This spicy fragrance has a long and rich heritage in Western ceremonial magick, and is especially important in Thelema. First described in The Book of Abramelin, a medieval German grimoire [1], it appears to be based on Holy Anointing Oil from Exodus [2]. It is one of the elements of the Cakes of Light which are provided to the congregation in the Gnostic Mass. E.G.C. [3] priests, priestesses, and bishops anoint themselves and others with it. Magicians use it in their personal rituals. It is mentioned by name in the Book of the Law [4]. Surely if ingredients matter anywhere, they matter here.

And yet, from translation to translation, the ingredients are not consistent. In addition, different traditions use different methods of preparation and different proportions, resulting in major differences in the oil's properties.

Most Abramelin oil available today uses Aleister Crowley's recipe [5], made by mixing the essential oils of myrrh, cinnamon, and galangal with a small amount of olive oil. This yields a highly concentrated oil that inflames the skin. Crowley's recipe is based on S.L.M. Mathers' translation of a French version of the Abramelin manuscript [6], with some changes to the proportions and the method of preparation. Mathers' translation, in turn, seems to be the only source for the use of galangal – he chose to translate 'Kalmus' as galangal rather than calamus, but gave no reason. He may well have intentionally changed the ingredient based on its symbolism, or he may have believed galangal to be a more accurate interpretation. Or he may have just made a mistake, we don't know. We do know that ceremonial magicians use Abramelin made from both these recipes to good effect, despite the differences.

I've chosen to make Abramelin oil from a different recipe. Based on modern analysis of the original manuscripts [7], it's probable that Abramelin oil originally included calamus and not galangal, and that it called for both cassia cinnamon and cinnamon verum. These changes make the scent more complex, and the symbolic correspondences shift. While still strongly scented, it's a milder oil that doesn't burn at all, thus removing one of Crowley's favorite effects [8]. So, is it still Abramelin if it doesn't follow Crowley? Is the more common recipe really Abramelin since it doesn't follow the original manuscripts? Will this oil have different properties than the other oil? Should O.T.O. rituals only use Abramelin made from Crowley's recipe? Does it matter?

Based on the care I've taken with my methods and ingredients, it certainly looks like it matters to me. But in fact, I don't really think ingredients are all that important. I just think they're fun.

A few years back I was discussing magick with a friend whom I greatly respect as a ceremonialist. He was talking about how much his personal practice had changed over the years. When he started out he'd been rigorous about having just the right tools, and only doing ritual at the right hours, on the right day. Especially,

Are Ingredients Important?

he said, he stressed over how to pronounce Barbarous Names. But over time all this fell away. He began to improvise, to use what came to hand, when he had time. His magick didn't suffer at all. The question in his mind was, would it have been just as good if he's started out free-form, or was this the natural evolution of a practicing magician? I was happy and intrigued to hear someone else describe the same arch in their practice that I'd followed in mine. Or as I put it then; "I used to think I had to have exactly the right woods and metals and symbols, and only used consecrated tools, after much preparation. But these days I can get the same results with pencil and paper, matches and whatever I can find in the yard."

I firmly believe that magick comes through the magician, not through the tools or the words or the calendar date. It's an internal faculty; in some a talent, in others a hard won skill. Great magicians, like all great artists, have both – they are born with talent and then work hard to develop their skills. So, if it all comes from within, if ingredients and tools and Names don't matter, why bother? Why in the world would anyone spend all that time and energy on the complicated and burdensome practice of ceremonial magick?

There are a lot of reasons. For starters, when I say that magick comes from the magician, I don't mean that's the only source. Nature is magick incarnate. In every plant and metal, every scent, in the vibration of every name, there are magical properties, energies that can be tapped into and shaped. Understanding these forces is essential to the process of learning to work with them, and working with them can make a world of difference. The tides of the seasons can lift us up and help us on our way, or can slow us down and make everything harder. When we use materials whose energies tend in the direction we want to go, those energies aid and strengthen us. Even though we manifest the magick, the entire unseen world is there to help and the wise magician learns where to find that help.

Still, these energies can be worked with through personal ritual and a wide variety of non-traditional methods. Why bother to follow the winding path of the ceremonial magician, studying obscure texts, memorizing and working the same old rituals until they are letter perfect, thinking about ingredients so much, you actually care whether "Calmus" meant *Acorus Calamus* or *Alpinia Galanga* to a Medieval German?

To me, it's art. Performing the Gnostic Mass hundredth time is like performing Macbeth or playing Bach. I didn't write it and can't change it, but I love to interpret it, and to work on the power of my performance. Familiarity is part of the power of these rituals – there's a deep well of stored potency and meaning in a ritual that has been worked over and over for years. I love the obscure and the complex for its own sake - a beautiful filigreed puzzle. Exploring whether a resin from Iran is better than a resin from Thailand is interesting in its own right. Will my ritual still work if I use them interchangeably? Sure. It'll probably work if I leave them out completely, although I may need to focus harder. On the flip side, an ingredient whose properties work against the ritual can be overcome, or ignored. But I avoid those situations as much as I can. Not because I think the ingredients create the magick, but because the right tools and scents and colors work with me to add grace and beauty and depth.

So, to answer my own question; No, ingredients don't really matter, magick can work without them. But is 'what works' the whole point? I'll have to say no to that as well. The right ingredients are among the tools we use for the perfection and embellishment of our Art. I may not need them, but I love them all the same.

References

[1] Although probably written in the early 15th century, the earliest surviving manuscript dates from about 1604: Wolfenbüttel Library, Codex Guelfibus 10.1.

[2] King James Bible, Exodus 30:23-25

[3] Ecclesia Gnostic Catholica. See http://oto-usa.org/egc.html.

[4] Crowley, Aleister. The Book of the Law: Liber Al Vel Legis, III 23.

[5] Crowley, Aleister. Magick: Book 4. (Weiser, 1997)

[6] Abraham of Worms, translated and edited by Mathers, S.L. MacGregor. *The Book of the Sacred Magic of Abramelin the Mage*. (1897; reprinted by Dover Publications, 1975)

[7] Abraham von Worms, edited by Dehn, Georg. *Buch Abramelin das ist Die egyptischen großen Offenbarungen. Oder des Abraham von Worms*

Are Ingredients Important?

Buch der wahren Praktik in der uralten göttlichen Magie. (Editions Araki, 2001).

Steven Guth's English translation of Dehn's work again translates calamus as galangal. See *Book of Abramelin: A New Translation* by Abraham von Worms, edited by Georg Dehn, translated by Steven Guth, foreword by Lon Milo DuQuette. (Nicholas Hays, 2006).

[8] "This oil is of a pure golden colour; and when placed upon the skin it should burn and thrill through the body with an intensity as of fire." Crowley, Aleister. Magick: Book 4.

Biography

Shellay Maughan has been a student of magick for over 40 years, and was one of the founders of the Dianic Women of the Goddess tradition. An ordained priestess in Ecclesia Gnostica Catholica, she is a dedicated member of Ordo Templi Orientis and Body Master of Horizon Oasis in Seattle, Washington.

THE ACTIVE AND THE RECEPTIVE: A NEW FORMULA FOR TALISMANIC MAGICK
KAYLA BLOCK

Death

Peter was in organ failure after a long struggle with a terminal illness. He'd been dying for years. But now, it wasn't a matter of months or weeks. It was a matter of days. It wasn't theoretical anymore.

The time for energy workings, healings, or attempts at divine intervention was long gone. I wanted a talisman but I couldn't find an appropriate formula.

Pain management? The doctors were on that.

Resolution of interpersonal issues? Peter had been dying for a long time. Whatever could be resolved, already was.

Peace for family members? They had their advance notice and had made their peace.

So, what kind of help would be useful? He wasn't entirely coherent. At times, he seemed to wonder where he might be going. At other times, he seemed to be hanging out with people that none of the rest of us could see. But in a moment of coherence, he said, "I'm dying, K."

"Yes Peter, you are."

"K, where do people go when they leave the hospital?"

"Peter, do you mean, when they die? Are you afraid? You will be okay, Peter."

He laughed and had nothing else coherent to say.

Death may be the biggest mystery. It's what drives us to religion, informs our spirituality, and sometimes keeps us awake at night with fear and worry.

Death is as mysterious as birth, yet we celebrate the latter and fear the former. We barely understand how we come into this world and we certainly don't understand how we leave it. Yet, it is all just time points in the cycle of life.

The Active and the Receptive

Death brings us full circle. In alchemy, a dead thing is imbued with life. Its impurities are removed. It becomes eternal and timeless (Crowley 1991). Death brings the union of all opposites. The union of the Sun and the Moon, the union of Human and God, the union of Venus and Mars. Visit the interior of the earth, and by rectifying, find the hidden stone.

From Solomon Trismosin's 1582 manuscript: "V.I.T.R.I.O.L. Visita Interiora Terrae Rectificando Invenies Occultum Lapidem" (JK 1920). Visit the interior of the earth, and in rectifying, discover the hidden stone. This is a formula for coming to terms with death. Visit the underworld of our own subconscious. Find the part of ourselves which is pure and eternal. This is the creation of the Solar or Subtle Body, the accomplishment of the Great Work, the Union of all Dyads, poured into the Cup of Babalon. This work allows us to cross over into death with conscious deliberation, as whole beings.

"Mors janua vitae. Vita janua mortis." Death is the gate of life. Life is the gate of death.

This was the seed that wanted to grow. These thoughts informed the working I wanted to do. But my seed idea was not substantial enough for me to figure out how to approach the working.

Now, I was getting somewhere. But how could I help Peter accomplish his own Great Work? Perhaps more importantly, I recognized that I needed to do something for myself to mark his death. Though I'd had years to mentally prepare, I was about to lose my best friend.

"It's all knowing what to start with. If you start in the right place and follow all the steps, you will get to the right end" (Moon 2003).

Talismans

A talisman is a unifying, physical embodiment of the Will of the Magician. Traditionally, the magician forces her Will upon the telesmatic material basis, invokes and evokes forces, and orders the spirits to go out and accomplish the task.

Throughout history, various methods for talismanic magick have been used. I'd worked with many of these methods with some great successes. I thought through methods I'd used.

The Golden Dawn attributed talismanic magick to the Hebrew letter Heh in the formula or name, YHShVH or Yehushua (Regardie 2002.) This is the four-fold, unspeakable name of God,

YHVH, with the descent of Spirit or Shin into the middle. The first Hebrew letter, Heh, in this formula, is attributed to the Cup of the magician, the recipient of the magician's energy. The cup is attributed to the emotions and feelings. As a physical cup catches and holds liquids, so a talisman can be viewed as catching and holding the magician's energies.

The Golden Dawn further elaborated on talismanic magick in a paper known as "Z-2: The Formulae of the Magic of Light: An Introduction to the Practical Working of the Z-2 Formula" (Regardie 2002). The Z-2 document instructs the magician in a method for putting a material basis through the Neophyte Golden Dawn ritual. The ceremony takes a dark, dead matter and imbues it with vitality and life force. The talismanic energy is then sent out to serve the magician's purpose.

The talisman can be made of any material basis. Divine forces are invoked, and a black cord and cloth are wrapped around the talismanic object to represent the robe of the Neophyte and the outer shell of darkness. The purpose of the working is stated, and the talisman is purified and consecrated by water and fire. God names are invoked and used to empower the talisman in its journey towards activation. Finally, the talisman is brought forth from darkness into light with these words, "Creature of Talismans, long hast thou dwelt in darkness. Quit the night and seek the day." (Regardie 2002) More invocations, consecrations, evocations, and demands are performed. The ceremony is long, complex, and involves significant planning and research.

This type of working can be used for material or spiritual gain but it requires having a firm grip on the intention of the operation. In this particular instance, I didn't have a solid formulation of what I needed. Commanding the spirits is a concept that has been around since the Renaissance. But I didn't know what I'd even want to command.

Austin Osman Spare and Peter Carroll devised a streamlined method of wish or sigil magick as an alternative to more ponderous forms of traditional talismanic magick by focusing the intent into an increasingly abstract symbol set. (Carroll 1987).

Carroll says that wishing isn't enough because the wish often ends up in a dialog with the mind. So a sigil magick operation involves:

- formulating the desired result
- creating a symbol of that desire

The Active and the Receptive

- losing the desire to the conscious mind
- charging the sigil

Aleister Crowley's Book of the Law advises, "For pure will, unassuaged of purpose, delivered from the lust of result, is every way perfect." (Crowley 1904)

A statement of magical intent is formulated using a simple sentence. Each duplicated letter is removed. Spare recommended using a format that starts with, "this my wish..." For example, THIS MY WISH TO ATTAIN AN A IN MY COLLEGE CLASS transforms to:

THISMYWOANMCLEG

The magician transforms the single letters into a stylized symbol that incorporates the letters of the wish. By focusing the Will of the magician in this manner, the desire becomes abstract and the lust of results is dissipated.

The sigil or talisman in this type of working usually takes place by an increase in focused sexual energy which is utilized to imbue the material form with the magician's own life force.

God-forms and entities are not generally invoked. There are no charges to the spirit, no purifications or consecrations, and the entire operation can be performed with a minimum of thought, time or tools.

I fondly call this type of magick "wankomancy" for the suggested method of charging the talisman by masturbation to orgasm. This type of working seems to be effective for gain of material things, but is more suited to mundane, rather than spiritual workings. It wasn't what I needed.

A Breakthrough

I needed a formula that thrust out the first whirlings of will. The Wand of the magician.

I needed to reflect and contain that whirling of Will, holding it in the magician's Cup to gain the understanding of the next step.

The thrusting forth of Will is the Yod of YHVH. The reflectivity and containment of that Will is the Cup of the magician, the first Heh of YHVH.

What if I took it to the next step of using the complete formula of YHVH? The Golden Dawn uses the first Heh in YHVH as the basis for talismanic magick. But the entire formula is creation, starting with a formless fire and finally grounded into earthly manifestation.

Vav is the sword of reason. It is that which tears things apart. How could this step fit into a working formula of talismanic magick? The Hebrew letter Vav means nail. It is the thing which binds two things together.

My next step became clear. Heh final is manifestation. It is the grounding, all the way down to earth, of that whirling of Will.

Yod. Heh. Vav. Heh.
Fire. Water. Air. Earth.
Will. Understanding. Reason. Manifestation.

I could see an emerging pattern of active and passive elements. I could see a calling forth and receiving.

I didn't need to know where I'd end up! All I needed was my seed. And the next step would be dictated by the previous step.

The Sun. There could be no better starting point than the Sun for a death working. The center, the balance point on the Tree of Life.

Yod. Fire. The Father. On the Tree of Life, it is Chokmah, or in English, "Wisdom." The letter Yod, in Hebrew, means "hand." Hands are how we interact with and grab into the world. It is the fist, expressive of Will. It is a declaration. It is the Fire of the Wands of the Tarot. It is the life force whose expression sets the world into motion. It is the masculine energy which shoots out into the world. When yod is added to a Hebrew word, it makes that word possessive. And so, it is the first statement of owning one's intention. The projection of the Will into the universe, into the material base, is of the nature of fire.

Heh. Water. The mother. On the Tree of Life, it is "Binah", or "Understanding." In Hebrew, Heh means "window", and the first expression of Heh in YHVH is the reflective Cup that catches the Fiery Will of the Yod. It is the Cup into which we pour our understanding. It is the receptive, female energy. It is the Cup of Babalon into which we pour the Fire of our Will to shape it with our Understanding.

Vav. Air. The Son. On the Tree of Life, it references "Tiphareth", or "Beauty." Vav means a "nail" in Hebrew. In YHVH, it partakes of the nature of Air. It is our reason. It is the Sword which divides and separates, therefore creating. For example, in the

Book of Genesis, God creates the world by separating the light from the dark, the heavens from the earth. And this demonstrates how Vav partakes of the nature of division, while also representing a union, as signified by the nail which binds two things together.

Heh final. Earth. On the Tree of Life, this references Malkuth, the earth or the "Kingdom." In the formula of YHVH, it references the daughter – the product of the union of the father, Chokmah, and the Mother, Binah. The Twin and the Lover of Vav. Heh final is of the earth.

YHVH.

The thrusting life force energy has been reflected, caught and contained in the cup of Heh, the mother. It has been used to unite and separate in the Vav or the Son. And then, the energy, the force of Will, is grounded and manifested in the Earth.

Hebrew Letter	Meaning	Family	Element	Weapon
Yod	Hand or Fist	Father	Fire	Wand
Heh	Window	Mother	Water	Cup
Vav	Nail	Son	Air	Sword
Heh (final)	Window	Daughter	Earth	Pantacle or Disk

The Working

Its father is the Sun and its mother the Moon. – The Emerald Tablet

I set up a solar temple. Every element, fire, water, air, earth, was represented in the microcosm of my temple. I formulated my material base of cardboard and paint. I put the colors and symbols of the Sun on one side. I left the obverse side blank. Lunar seemed like it might be the next step, but I decided to ask and listen instead of impose and force.

The Sun is the stellar representative of our very life force. Its cycles control our harvests, our seasons. The rising and the setting of the Sun's cycles has been used to represent the human cycles of life and death for millennia.

The Sun doesn't really change. It is always as it is. But from our vantage point on the Earth, it appears to die and be reborn on a daily basis.

I wanted the warmth of the Sun's rays to always shine on Peter. I wanted him to live as the Sun lives, eternal and glorious. I wanted to wrap him in star-stuff.

I called forth the Solar Gods. I asked for their assistance. I called forth my own life force, my own Solar Body and focused it down into a laser sharp point. I thrust it forth into the talismanic material base.

This was the Yod, my hand, declaring my Will.

And then, I did something different than anything I'd ever read in a book or done before.

I listened.

I became the Cup. I became the reflective material and opened myself up to the impressions of what came back.

This was the work of the Wand and the work of the Cup. My elemental weapons, my magick, were formulating themselves in a new way.

The next steps pointed me to the union of that dyad. The lunar aspect of our lives is also cyclical. The moon rises and sets, and waxes and wanes. Just as the Sun only appears to change, the Moon is always the same. It just looks different to us from our perspective on Earth. It reaches its ripe glory in the full moon and becomes quietly invisible in the phase of the New Moon.

I wanted the delicate moonlight to always caress his cheek. I wanted his waning to be just the beginning of another cycle. And as the cycles of the Moon and Sun were mysteries to the Ancients, so are the cycles of Life and of Death mysteries to us, even now.

I created a Lunar temple and painted symbols and colors of the Moon on the obverse side.

This was my Heh, the Mother who joins in union with Yod, the Father. A catching and containment of Will, and a time to reflect.

The wind has borne it in its body, and the earth has nourished it. – *The Emerald Tablet.*

Vav is the Hebrew letter that means "nail." This step is a paradox because Vav is also attributed to the sword and dispersion. It is the very essence of division. And yet, through division, God created the World in the book of Genesis. And without division, there is no-thing.

Vav is division and it is the union of the Father and Mother. The nail binds two disparate things into one unity. It is the coalescence of the dyad into the One. It is how I willed to create this talisman. The division of the Sun and Moon become that One Thing.

There were no paintings or colors for this part. It was a purely internal experience, accompanied by incantations.

Grounding the energy into Heh Final, or Earth, was simply a declaration and a rap of my fist. "So mote it be."

This is the whole most strong strength of all strength, for it overcomes all subtle things, and penetrates all solid things.

Thus was the world created.

-- Emerald Tablet

The End

I don't know what impact this working had on Peter. He seemed to have been at peace. But within 24 hours of the working, he was completely incoherent and within 48 hours, he was dead. I dreamed of him the night he died. I dreamed he was scared and flailing and trying to hold onto me. And I dreamed that he nearly drowned me.

The phone call came that morning.

Whether the working brought Peter any peace is not anything I can know. But it brought me peace.

And after he died, I took the talisman and burned it, scattering the ashes to the ocean and saying my goodbyes. But I kept one tiny part for myself. And maybe that's all any of us can really ask for.

Peter's been dead for more than 15 years. But I have had many occasions to utilize this YHVH formula of talismanic magick. This method respects and even requests input from the forces that are being worked and that is a different approach. There is no ordering around of spirits, nor is there any binding or compelling them to my Will. There is a dialog.

I use it for workings where the goal is unclear. I use it when I want to speak to and listen to the Gods. I use it when I'm uncertain. And I use it even if I think I'm certain but want to allow a response to my Will.

References

Carroll, Peter (1987). *Liber Null & Psychonaut: An Introduction to Chaos Magic.* York Beach, Maine: Weiser.

Crowley, Aleister (1904). *The Book of the Law*. http://lib.oto-usa.org/libri/liber0220.html (1991). *Magick in Theory and Practice*. New York: Magickal Childe Publishing, Inc.

Moon, Elizabeth (2003). *The Speed of Dark*. New York: Del Rey.

Regardie, Israel (2002). *The Golden Dawn*. St. Paul, MN: Llewellyn.

JK (1920) *Splendor Solis, Alchemical Treatises of Solomon Trismosin Adept and Teacher of Paracelsus*. London: Kegan Paul.

Biography

Kayla Block is a Thelemite who just celebrated her 20th year as an initiate in Ordo Templi Orientis (OTO.) She is an ordained Priestess in Ecclesia Gnostica Catholica, a trained initiator, and is the Secretary of the Education Committee for United States Grand Lodge of OTO, facilitating the development of curricula in Thelema and the Western Mystery traditions.

RADICAL FEMINIST ALCHEMY
HELEN HONEYCUTT

My name is Helen and I am a radical feminist alchemist....

And what makes me a radical feminist alchemist? Well, whenever I start to talk about my alchemical work I invariably get to the point where someone asks me 'what about Jung?" and I used to wince and cringe. Not because I had anything horribly negative to say about Jung, but because Jung wasn't an alchemist. Jung was either a psychologist, a psychiatrist, or a philosopher, depending on who you ask, but he definitely was not an alchemist. How, you may ask can I say such a horrible thing? Easy enough to answer: there is no indication that Jung invested in glassware, went on long trips to swamps and other gooey locations, or had heavy metal poisoning. What he did do was follow in the footsteps of a privileged group that I tend to refer to as "renaissance white boys". While I myself am white enough to glow in the dark, my outraged feminist sensibilities definitely abhor the transformation of alchemy from one of the few professions legally allowed to women in the European middle ages to the preserve of dilettante philosophers and Ponzi scam specialists. It all started you see, with the feminist origins of alchemy.

The dim origins of alchemy as a profession preclude any authoritative proclamations about womens' role in those origins, but there are hints, here and there, of alchemy as 'womens' work'. The work that leads to alchemy are some of the essential occupations engaged in by women in most early cultures - the collection, preservation, and preparation of food and drink, the preparation of fiber for clothing and shelter, and the preparation of medical remedies. The homely origins are in baking and brewing, weaving and dying, birthing the young and easing the dying. Technological innovation is not a new process, it is the sometimes serendipitous product of daily survival.

Look, for instance, at our daily bread. The process of daily bread production is enormously complicated when viewed from its origins. Unprocessed grain is nearly inedible by humans, it requires significant processing to get to the usable whole grain, and requires yet more preparation before consumption. To find and harvest, dry and thresh wild grain is incredibly time and labor intensive, waste would be abhorrent, and so the war against vermin and spoilage would need to be waged. After cultivation began there would be yet more time and energy devoted the product, in plowing and planting and watering and protection from wandering herbivores and marauding neighbors, and then on to the real work of threshing, grinding, mixing and baking. How long ago did some woman find her carefully hoarded grain had gotten damp and sprouted, and made the decision to dry it out on a hot rock and grind it up anyway? When did a bowl of leftover gruel catch a yeast and provide beer for breakfast or crackers that rose to become chewy? And having occurred how rapidly did word pass from woman to woman - here was a new and innovative technique, a better product, a technology not previously used. Women had to be observant to survive, so it would not be long before someone started using alcohol as a fixative, and extractive, and solvent, and preservative and medicine, and the elder women would mess around with dye plants and ferment weird combinations, dip in some wool and hang it up 'just to see what I get'. Eventually the beer would improve, and someone's yeast or grain would become popular, and be traded down the river and over the hill, and she would share the proceeds with her sister, who was cooking and cleaning for two homes so that more beer could be sold. Or special yeast, or wine, or dye, or aspirin, or plant extracts, or saltpeter, or chalk, or medicinal clay, or honey, or....And alchemy in the ancient world became industrial chemistry and compounding pharmacy in the modern world, but first it had to get past the Renaissance.

The Renaissance is the period when a middle class was coalescing, and disposable income and inherited wealth not tied to agriculture or military service became more common. Men of a certain income and social class had acquired a new thing - leisure time, and they wanted to take it out for a spin. What seems to have happened is that these amateur philosophers pre-dated Jung by a couple of centuries in co-opting the vocabulary of alchemy to describe, metaphorically, spiritual and psychological processes, and they also developed an odd sort of mnemonic process where going through the physical procedures in tandem with spiritual exercises produced some item as a byproduct of spiritual growth.

This odd amalgamation had some very practical results, not the least of which is that it allowed lay people to discuss matters formerly the sole domain of the church without being denounced as heretics. You could develop a series of spiritual exercises, dabble in spiritualism, use a variety of techniques, such as scrying, and generally practice both thaumaturgy and a limited theurgy without fear of persecution, as long as you had some odd looking glassware burbling foul smelling vapors in the background. All of this would have been merely an odd side-trip in history if it hadn't been for the three G's- greed, gullibility, and gold.

Enter the Ponzi scheme- and the downfall of alchemy as a respectable profession. It seems to be a failing of human nature that there persists a belief in 'free lunch'. Modern physics declares the laws of conservation of mass and energy, and such applies to all endeavors- yet despite both knowledge and good sense the hope of free lunch springs eternal.

So it was with the traveling alchemist' show, where a very charismatic guy and his assistant showed up in town and offered to produce 'gold from base metal', for a small fee, of course, not much really, just to cover supplies, and maybe a little over to cover living expenses etc....And people with more money than sense invested in these schemes, and brought their friends in, and as is usual with many victims of fraud were too embarrassed to cop to their gullibility, thereby letting the scam continue fifty miles down the road. Poof! Alchemy as a profession was burnt toast on a stick, and the several related professions got a sudden surge in overqualified workers. It was a lot like hiring Bayer's research fellows to sell aspirin at the local discount drug emporium.

Real alchemists were suddenly physicians, or apothecaries, or bakers, or brewers, or dye merchants-and all of these were guild occupations restricted to men. Women were out the door or at least shoved over to doing the grueling work to produce items whose profit went not to them, but to the men they worked for, be they relatives, spouses, or owners. It was a crushing blow economically and legally for women professionals, who had already been shoved out of teaching, law, medicine from surgery all the way down to professional nursing, trade of all kinds including professional status in kitchen and weaving shed, all of the decorative and textile arts, and public performing arts. The last profession left was prostitution, and it paid badly, had lousy working conditions, and was physically taxing, not to mention usually costing a hefty percentage of the gross back to whatever male was renting out the space and putative protection. (Women's economic opportunities are remarkably similar over time, aren't they?)

So where does that leave me as a modern feminist alchemist? Well, I spend a lot of time at needlework or weaving, and I bake a lot of bread, and can, bottle and jar a lot of produce, and mix up a variety of potions and tinctures and elixirs for my medically indigent friends. I haunt thrift stores and antique sales for oddly shaped glassware and really obscure books of recipes and formulas and every time I get out my crockpot or double boiler I say a blessing on the soul of Maria the Jewess, (nobody's sure if she was Jewish or just a really smart lady from the Mediterranean area) who was revered as the mother of alchemy, but now is remembered for the bain-marie (Maria's bath)- the humble but essential double-boiler. And I search for the voices of modern women like Yvonne Young Tarr, who in 1972 fervently described baking bread - but to me she was speaking of real alchemy, and baking was the metaphor.

Baking is not an art, it is an act of creation....in the act of creating bread, an honest loaf, an object with a presence, a fragrance, a substance, a taste, some would even say a soul, the baker has changed grain and flour and liquid into and entity. She has taken yeast, a dormant colony of living plants, and released and nurtured them in embryonic warmth, had sprinkled in sugar, on which yeast thrives, has sifted in flour that builds the cellular elastic structure that holds the tiny carbon dioxide bubbles that raise the framework of the house called BREAD. And in this house is love, and warmth, and nourishment, and comfort, and care, and caring, and taking care, and time gone by, and time well spent, and things natural, and things good, and honest toil, and work without thought of reward, and all of these things once had, now lost in a country and a world that has rushed by itself and passed itself running and never noticed its loss.

Biography

Helen Adams Honeycutt was born in the then small oil town of Bakersfield, CA. The grand-daughter and daughter of avid gardeners, she began practicing herbalism as a teenager, which then blossomed into a love of alchemy. She started practicing the craft shortly thereafter and has been a high priestess for over 20 years. She lives in Bremerton, WA. where she spends her time around her great family and friends.

DESIRE - THE SEEKER
KAT SANBORN

Writing about myself and my spiritual path sounded easy. I would find some facile language for my current state of magical, physical and emotional health.

I could not have been more wrong.

It has been like tearing the scab off of a not quite healed wound and as I had discovered, there were a lot of tender places.

I came back into contact with the loneliness and isolation that defined my teens and twenties.

Slipping on the polished mask of my thirties changed nothing. I looked better, and talked a good game, but inside I felt hollow and sought to fill that void as always with various remedies.

I became fascinated by the occult at an early age.

From the first moment I can remember, I have had an awareness of a divine presence – within and without. This was both inspiring and emotionally painful. I sought truth and wisdom and when I could not find it, sought oblivion.

Burdened with a wide self-destructive streak, I engaged in risky behaviors that make me glad now that I survived. Life is precious, but for a long time I didn't know that.

Taught to read at three, I could identify almost any animal, bird or insect and could often recall their Latin names. My parents were proud of their gifted child.

I was strictly brought up – attending parochial school until high school. My mother was a debutante, and as a young girl I did wear gloves and shiny black Mary Jane shoes with bright white socks.

I was taught how to set a table, to curtsy and write thank-you notes. I have never said a curse word in front of my mother or rested my elbows on her table.

The only books we children were allowed to read aside from the Disney or Reader's Digest series were educational.

A stick-figure little girl, it was not easy to find clothes for me, much less school uniforms. The nuns dressed me in the smallest uniform skirt. Once they let go after fastening it, the skirt fell to the floor. My parents had to buy me a different skirt that was approved to be a proper and modest garment.

Because of this difference, I was ignored by the children at school. I soon learned the advantages in blending in with the environment and also learned to do the same in other places. I was often seated on the floor unnoticed in the same room with adults during their conversations. As long as I made no eye contact, I could usually remain under the radar.

In this life, my mother's old-fashioned expectation was that when grew up, I would not attend college, but would marry and have children.

Marriage and having children never looked like the best deal to me at the time.

My parents divorced when I was young. Dad seemed to have all of the freedom in the world and plenty of ladyfriends.

My mother had four children all under the age of ten to care for on her own. She had some friends and dated seldom. Being the eldest, I learned early on to feed, bathe, dress and be responsible for my two brothers and sister. Mom got a job handing guard dogs at night, and slept during the day while we were at school.

I was sheltered, restless, and depressed. I had little relationship with my parents and few friends.

Attending parochial school meant being in church at least twice per week for years. This gave me ample opportunity to observe the congregation as the people heard sermons, sang, and participated in seasonal celebrations.

Many around me seemed to know his or her God. I could feel a divine presence, yet I couldn't find words or outside definitions for what I understood to be true.

I felt like an outsider to the spiritual world – and I wanted in.

I started reading about every spiritual tradition I could get information on. Whatever the Oxnard Public Library had to offer or could get, I read.

I became conversant in the Dewey Decimal system, sometimes flipping through the cards to find and write down titles. Books I wasn't allowed to check out yet because I was too young, I read standing in the aisle.

What I discovered was that not only was I not a Christian and never would be, but that within all of the different spiritual traditions I read about – I could see that they were all real and valid to their devotees. The world was full of people who could see and feel God each in their own way.

Each tradition had its own unique beauty, blending in with my growing awareness of the spiritual worldview.

Desire - The Seeker

The only thing I knew absolutely is that God existed, that I was part of the Body of God and that I would one day find answers or at least a road toward them and possibly, other people like me.

As I grew from a girl into a woman I discovered a powerful word – desire.

This word seemed to be defining factor in most people's lives whether they were conscious of it or not. A dangerous word. One that is not always mentioned but definitely part of the conversation.

Remember the first time that you felt real desire?

Even if you couldn't see the object of your desire, you could smell it, taste it and feel the warmth of its breath on your cheek. It woke up with you in the morning, was with you all day, and reminded you of its presence just as you fell asleep and dreamed. Often your desire would enter and inform your dreams, changing your interior landscape and by extension the potential physical manifestation of your world.

This is how much I wanted to know divinity deeply – to have the light of the gnosis permeate my entire being. As my awareness of this deep desire grew– so also the desire for connection and communion.

I kept reading, explored and experienced as I walked the earth. The people I was surrounded by as seemed to not feel this hard-driving need to know. My friends seemed content to work, enjoy recreation, and a variety of relationships.

I didn't do any of those things more than was strictly necessary. How much do I confess? I confess that I was unhappy and took what I believed at the time to be viable steps and remedies to relieve that deep sorrow. Suffice it to say, these short-term measures did not solve any problems, only created more unrest.

It was in my thirties that I found where I wanted to be, and became an initiate of OTO.

Attending my first Gnostic Mass, I felt like I was finally in a place where it felt to me that the potential was here for me to find truth revealed. One of the things that have learned as an initiate is that truth is always being revealed, but that there are no easy answers. Spiritual development in my case became more difficult, but the sense of accomplishment and a journey that has real and lasting value cannot be equaled.

A decade later, I am still immersed in my personal work and my involvement in the OTO is a lifetime commitment. At various times I have been fully involved, doing Order work on a daily basis to the far side of taking blocks of time to devote myself to my personal life.

On this path the movement has been constant and sometimes hectic but I wouldn't have it any other way. I am surrounded by people doing their Will. What better inspiration to do my own?

Initiation for me has been a process of reconciling the inner landscape with the outer world.

Today, the world is fascinating place full of Light, Life, Love and Liberty. Upon this reflection, I am really glad to be here. I am truly fortunate.

The amazing vibrancy, color, and light my Brethren add to my life cannot be described in mundane words. It is something that has to be experienced in order to be understood.

The world had always been an amazing and magical place as a child. What happens to us that we lose the belief that all is possible? This belief is the engine that drives us with force and fire to accomplish those things we hold dearest. To not give up.

Isn't it often true that we are brought up to understand that when we reach our majority or so-called "age of reason" that we are to lessen, then lose our childlike wonder and excitement? I couldn't wait to grow up so that I could stop having meat loaf for dinner. No other plans aside from that and finding the ineffable Name of God.

And isn't it also true that as we gain practical, worldly experience, our awareness of subtle phenomena is to fade away, along with the stars in our eyes?

The world does not have to lose its color and music as we mature; it is more that we add our own special imprimatur to the pages of our lives.

We have the constant ability to change our fortunes and future if we take the first important step of believing that we can by harnessing the power of our personal Will. This effort puts us squarely within the magical current and functioning in our particular contribution to the physical and spiritual world.

Biography

Kat Sanborn has been is a lifelong student of the arcane and occult and an initiate of the OTO for over a decade. She has held a variety of positions within the Order, both on the local and national levels. in addition to being a chartered OTO initiator, she is an Ordained Priestess of Eccleisia Gnostica Catholica. She resides in California.

SATANISM - THE LEFT HAND PATH

Women on the Left Hand Path confront several challenges - the general stereotyping of Satanists in a Christian culture, the stereotyping of Satanic women as shrewish, and additionally, the stereotyping of women within the Left Hand Path as sexually available vamps. Venus Satanas finds strength in her own unmediated relationship with Satan. Sybil Black draws on demonized images of women's independence to claim power for women on the path.

MY LIFE IN SATANISM
VENUS SATANAS

I am Venus Satanas. My interests are the occult, the practice of magic, and the path of Satanism. In the 90's my discovery of Satanism and occult began at the local library. Waiting for me on the shelf was a hardcover book titled *The Church of Satan* by Blanche Barton. I read it several times, and identified with many of the values of Satanism that were presented in this book.

From this, I created a pact with Satan. My pact was an initiation and it is part of my spirituality, and an agreement to be allied with Satan, for our mutual benefit.

My interests in magic are eclectic witchcraft and ritual magic. I am an independent spiritual Satanist, and I do not belong to any organizations. In my magical work now, I am exploring the benefits of Planetary energies. Along with this, I enjoy using candle spells and sigil magic. In the past I had experimented with Chaos magic through authors like Peter Carroll and Phil Hine, and I have used the rituals from the Satanic Bible. I have also created my own personal rituals for magic. In 2004, I created a website, where my writings about Satanism and magic have inspired others to find their own path.

In my practices, creating my own method of magic, eclectic in style, has been beneficial for me, rather than to follow a tradition or specific path that is already established in the mainstream practices of magic. In my experience, to create one's own method is the Satanic way.

In 2004, I renewed my pact with Satan, after leaving a bad 7 year relationship. I moved out and got my own place, and adopted a cat from the shelter for a companion. At my new apartment doorstep a single pink rose was growing. What influenced me to create my magical name, was this symbol of the rose, and what it had represented to me. The rose represented a new life, and also it was the symbolic of the Goddess, Venus. This name was created from the symbolic events that were in my life at the time that lead me to realize that 'I am a woman, and I am a Satanist, I am Venus Satanas!'.

While Venus is not traditionally a Satanic goddess figure, she represents qualities and attributes that can be appreciated by

Satanists. Venus is the passion and love for life that is a requirement for good Satanic living. She also represents pleasure, enjoyment, ecstasy, and desire, as both virtues and vices. This goddess was also associated with Lucifer. In Roman mythology Venus and Lucifer were both symbolized by the eastern star. Lucifer is recognized as the fallen angel who is associated with Satan in some Christian and Satanic beliefs. But the Satan of Christianity is much different than the ideas and beliefs about Satan that emerged from Satanism. This Satanism as a philosophy and religion started around the same time of the other neo-occult groups and New Religious Movements in the middle of last century.

Satanists are very diverse and individual in our beliefs and ideals. Organized Satanism offers specific beliefs and practices. I have found in my studies that a lot of Satanists prefer solitary work. I prefer this as well and I am independent with my practices. Although as Satanists we all do not share the same interests, the one thing that we do have in common is Satan, and whether that force is recognized as spiritual or symbolic is up to the individual.

As a Satanist, Theistic Satanism is my path. Theistic Satanism is the recognition of Satan as a god. Amongst those who identify with Theistic Satanism, there is no one singular definition or consensus as to who or what Satan represents. It may be a form of polytheistic worship for some, including other deities and gods into religious worship.

Satanism as a social movement appeared in 1966 with the creation of the Church of Satan and Anton LaVey. Satanism emerged from the "occult subculture with the formation of the Church of Satan" and expanded after the disbandment of the grottos in the seventies(Lewis 2001). Satanism is a very diverse practice, containing many beliefs. It is known that "Religious Satanism exists primarily as a decentralized subculture, not unlike the Neopagan subculture" (Lewis 2001). There are many different methods of Satanism, starting with basic dabbling, to Satanists that have Christian beliefs, Theistic Satanists, and those who are atheist, symbolic, or philosophical Satanists.

Prior to this emergence of Satanism in the last century, there was only a fantasy history created by Christian authors and church leaders, a type of propaganda which has lasted for centuries. Unfortunately, there are those that accept these prosecutions, hoaxes, witch trials, and fictional stories as fact, and they consider Satanism to be centuries old. The Satanism practiced today is a part of the New Religious Movement that developed within the last century.

Many Satanists have come from a Christian background, and many have used it as a transitory practice or belief. Some began in their teens with dabbling. It is for this reason that Satanists have gained a reputation for being a part of teenage rebellion, and have been disregarded by the occult community in the past. Most religious academics have not paid serious attention to Satanism, even though it has been established for nearly thirty years.

While women are not forgotten or ignored in Satanism, we definitely face stereotyping in a very specific way. The fact is, that most Satanists are male, as shown in a small survey conducted on Satanists in 2001, "One hundred and one survey respondents were male, thirty six were female" (Lewis 2001).

While women are not actively excluded from Satanic practices, the Satanic philosophy does not seem to appeal to very many women because of what it generally represents. The philosophies of Satanism are focused on the self and the ego, and self-worship, and this may not be appealing to women, because it is in contrast to the general social role of women as caretakers in society. Satanism is a path of personal power and the ego - and these are the things that have traditionally been associated with the masculine. This philosophy is represented by the flesh, the strength of the body, the ego, and the will.

The majority of current Satanic authors are men. Most of the organizations or groups that identify strictly with Satan or Satanism are created and organized by men, with only a few notable exceptions. For many years there has been a lot of aggression and in-fighting between these people at times, because Satanism is by nature an adversarial path.

Regardless of this, women are not excluded, or considered to be weak or insignificant in Satanism. It is the individual nature of Satanism that potentially makes this path appeal to all genders, as a form of self-empowerment. In order to understand women's role in Satanism, it's important to look at the history of how women fulfilled their role in this esoteric art.

The power of the feminine is generally represented by sexuality. Unlike other occult practices which may symbolize the feminine as the source of creation, in Satanism these aspects are mostly related to sex and pleasure. An example of this tradition can be seen in the footage of the LaVey Black Mass, a sexually charged ritual that shows a woman worshiped as the altar. While the priestess is laying naked upon the altar, and is the focus of attention, the male participants are robed. Woman was to serve as a symbol of man's lust and desires, and the pleasures of the flesh.

According to LaVey's description in the *Satanic Bible*, the Black Mass was a ritual that was performed by heretics and excommunicated priests of the Church that were divested of their holy powers. He tells of a lurid scene of degradation and blasphemy that was meant to mock the Church with a lustful ritual. The Black Mass used candles, the chalice, the "consecrated host", a priest, and assistants. After the ritual Satan would appear to bless the unholy congregation with the "kiss of shame".

> The popular concept of the black mass is thus: a defrocked priest stands before an altar consisting of a nude woman, her legs spread-eagled and vagina thrust open, each of her outstretched fists grasping a black candle made from the fat of unbaptized babies, and a chalice containing the urine of a prostitute (or blood) reposing on her belly...A triangular hosts of ergot-laden bread or black-stained turnip are methodically blessed as the priest dutifully slips them in and out of the altar-lady's labia. Then, we are told, an invocation to Satan and various demons is followed by an array of prayers and psalms chanted backwards or interspersed with obscenities...(LaVey 1976).

This was, of course, the Christian interpretation of the Black Mass that was likely inspired by fictional tales and witch-hunt confessions. According to LaVey, the feminine in this ritual also represented the Satanic "Chalice of Ecstasy". This chalice was filled with what was called the "Elixir Of Life", that was first drunk by the priest, then the assistant, and then passed to the participants.

The tradition was continued by LaVey in his version of the Mass, by sexually objectifying women and making them a source of sexual fascination and an object of worship during Satanic ritual. By doing this, he was promoting the worship of the flesh, the ideal of woman as the source of evil, and the feeling of lust directed by the Devil. Satanism is by definition a "religion of the flesh" (LaVey 1971). The Black Mass of Satanists seemed to glorify women in their physical form.

According to LaVeyan Satanism, all women are witches and have the potential to exert power and control over men, by using their sexual prowess and the willingness to dress in a suggestive manner, and to persuade through sexuality. Of course, LaVey developed these ideas during an era where people began to express more sexual freedom than ever before, so it seemed natural to idealize the female form upon the altar as a symbol of lust, by serving as a shocking symbol of sexual freedom and liberation.

Today the tradition of serving as an altar may continue as a form of empowerment for some Satanic women. However, this is an optional practice in Satanism. Not all women Satanists want to or have to serve only as an altar or as the assistant to the High Priest.

At my website I have argued against the sexual inequalities that the system of LaVeyan Satanism has presented to the public. In LaVey's book *The Compleat Witch*, witchcraft is described as a form of low sexual magic that women can take advantage of. Low magic in this instance is the use of psychology and sexuality for manipulation towards personal ends (LaVey 1971).

Some Satanic feminists who defend LaVey's view, say that Satan should represent the dominant and willful force in a woman's life (Barton 1997). LaVeyan Satanists speak of independence for women in Satanism, thinly veiled behind the transparent, sexual personality of the "Satanic Witch" who was glorified by LaVey. LaVey gives the highest regard for what he believes is lowest form of magic, a woman's sexuality.

I also believe that LaVey's categorization of women as the source of evil was an attempt to negate the movement of feminist Wiccan witchcraft which had gained in popularity during that era of New Religious Movements. It was suggested that instead of worshiping the goddess like pagan or witchcraft religions, the Satanist should worship herself, or be worshiped by man. Similar to Crowley, LaVey's methods of ritual served to shock and outrage the public and give them something that they wanted at the same time - entertainment. This is all a part of the foundation of the ideology of Satanism today.

The main instrument of magic in the Satanic ceremony is the sword or the dagger. This symbol traditionally represents the masculine and active forces of nature in many paths of magic, and serves as a symbol of authority, war and domination. LaVeyan Satanism is not based on spirituality, but within the *Satanic Bible*, the four crown Princes of Hell serve as the four directionals and the elements. This arrangement, inspired by *The Book of the Sacred Magic of Abra-Melin the Mage* (Mathers 1998), represents the four directionals and elements that are used in Satanic ritual. There is Belial, Lucifer, Leviathan, and Satan, all of which are not traditionally associated with feminine energies.

This is only one arrangement of deities and representations in Satanism, among many that are possible. For spiritual and Theistic Satanists, like myself, there is a different approach that is in contrast to the physical worship of symbolic Satanism. Some of us have associated directions and elements to represent all of the forces of nature, both masculine and feminine, positive and negative. For example, some Satanists revere Baphomet, and worship this force as a god and goddess all at once.

Other sects of Theistic satanism have adopted the worship of Lilith, Hecate, Kali, and other demonesses and Goddesses like them, as a representation of the Satanic feminine. A kind of dark feminism is entwined within the magic and psychology of Satanism. I want others to know that in Satanism, witchcraft is not only used by women. I have tried to observe this balancing factor of gender and energies in my personal rituals that I have performed. At my website, I am also formulating a ritual magic and eclectic witchcraft system for other Satanists that is gender neutral, so that it reaches to all audiences, not just male or female.

In my studies I have been inspired by the works of Diane Vera. It is Diane, and a few others online, who have made Theistic Satanism a well known alternative to LaVeyan Satanism. She is an outspoken Theistic Satanist, and Satanic Feminist, who has gained a reputation in the occult for her excellent writings. She claimed that if LaVey represented the age of Satan, then now, with the many freedoms available for women, is the "Age of Lilith". I love her enthusiasm. I have to agree that now more than ever, because of our opportunities, it's a great time in history to be a woman.

Satanism promotes freedom of thought and choice and because of this, there are issues and choices that I support, such as gay marriage. People should be able to live their lives according to their desires, and what makes them fulfilled as humans. It is wrong that the moral right wants to restrict the basic human right to love one another. I am also pro-choice, as I believe that women should be able to choose their own destiny.

There are perhaps many in Satanism who agree with these views. But there are only a few that are outspoken about these issues, which are so important in today's society.

While LaVeyan Satanism can be limiting when it comes to representing feminine forces, other spiritual paths of Satanism are exploring the feminine nature of Satanic expression. It is my feeling that magic, witchcraft, and satanism are not gender specific; anyone can benefit from these practices.

Since I have been involved with this project, *Women's Voices in Magic*, writing my essay has given me this opportunity to explore the important role of Women in magic and occultism I have also learned about the truths and realities of gender inequality in Satanic practice. It is my belief that Satan, when represented as god of this earth, and god of human desires, encompasses the qualities of all genders, and all people.

References

Barton, Blanche (1997). "Satanic Feminism", *The Black Flame* 6, 1-2. http://www.churchofsatan.com/Pages/Satfem.html

Lewis, James R. (2001). "Who Serves Satan? A Demographic and Ideological Profile." *Marburg Journal of Religion*, Volume 6, 2, June 2001.

Martin J.V., narrator (2006). *Hell, The Devil's Domain* [Television broadcast]. The History Channel.

Mathers, S.L. MacGregor, editor (1998). *The Book of Sacred Magic of Abramelin the Mage*. Montana: Kessinger.

LaVey, Anton (1971). *The Compleat Witch: or What to do When Virtue Falls*. New York, Dodd, Mead and Company.

LaVey, Anton (1976). *The Satanic Bible*. New York, Avon.

Satanas, Venus (2009). "Satanic Witchcraft" (online), accessed 5/6/09.http://www.spiritualsatanist.com/articles/magick/satanicwitchcraft.html

Vera, Diane (2003). "Infernal names, directional correspondences" (online), accessed 5/6/09. http://www.theisticsatanism.com/rituals/standard/names.html

Biography

Venus Satanas has been a Satanist since 1992, after she discovered Satanism at the local library when she found a book on the Church of Satan. This book inspired her to walk the left-hand path. She created a ritual dedication to Satan and to Satanism at the age of thirteen. She studied and practiced Satanism and various forms of witchcraft and magic.

Venus created her website, SpiritualSatanist.com, to share her ideas and experiences with other Satanists and seekers of the left hand path. Venus Satanas also produces videos at YouTube since 2007, with many subscribers [currently over 3,000!] who are interested in learning about the Occult and Satanism. Venus also has a personal blog, Spiritual Satanist where she posts information about Satanism and the occult. In 2009, Venus opened the Satanas Shop, to showcase and sell her Satanic art and merchandise all over the world.

She has also produced a video, "Spiritual Satanism", and the research book "The Al-Jilwah for Satanists", both published by Lulu. And, in 2009 Venus performed an evocation of Infernal Ones for the CD, "Masters of Invocation", produced by Jordan James.

Venus Satanas is an independent Satanist, and she does not belong to any organizations. She is the co-owner of HISS, the Horde of Independent Satanists, a Satanic knowledge resource for those who are not part of group or organized Satanism.

WOMEN AND THE LEFT HAND PATH
SYBIL BLACK

In the Western esoteric tradition, the term "Left-Hand Path" has come to be associated with the frequently demonized or even diabolized aim of the "non-union" of individual consciousness with, or even "separation from," the cosmos. (Flowers 1997)

Tantric Origins

The ultimate origins of the term, however, are Tantric, and its foundation in Hindu Tantra is critical to the present discussion. "Vama Marga" is the distinctly "left-hand" path of Tantra as opposed to the "Dakshina Marga" or "right-hand" path. This left-Hand path of Hindu Tantra is differentiated from the right by one overwhelming aspect: it necessitates the inclusion and worship of the Shakti, the female sexual godhead, in a physical form. Vama Marga Tantra also includes other practices considered taboo from the perspective of the Dakshina practitioner, but its main qualifier is that the male practitioner must unify with a woman, in a fashion which holds the female practitioner in high reverence. An example of this, among many, is that the Lingam, or male organ, may only be inserted into the Yoni, or female organ in a position in which the woman in on top, which is significant "because it is always the case in Hindu Tantric tradition that woman is the embodiment of Shakti, the embodiment of essence, purity, divinity,the energetic principal, Goddess incarnate" (Michaels and Johnson 2006). The term Vama can also refer to the female breast, in which case the term roughly means "female-path". Kali, an aspect of the Shakti often called the "black Goddess of Wisdom," and one who is frequently associated with western Left Hand Path (LHP) practices, is worshipped by both branches of Tantra through poetry evocative of the cremation ground and other aspects of a darker spirituality, as in this poem by the 18th century Tantrika Ramprasad:

Mysterious Ma Kali,
cremation grounds are your great delight,
for there you release souls from mundane experience.
I have transformed my heart into a cremation ground

*so you will be attracted here to dance
as flames of liberating bliss.*

*O wisdom Goddess,
my limited desire has been consumed
on the blazing pyre of renunciation.
O Goddess of Freedom,
I am surrounded by the ashes
that were my assumptions,
waiting ardently for you to come.
Please manifest in the brilliant midnight hour
of this renouncing heart.*
(Hixon and Sinha 1994)

Here the "corrupting"influence of the cremation ground, a place of great taboo for its filth and pollution, is the place of redemption for the Tantrik initiate.

The origins of Tantra in India are thought to be in goddess worship dating back to a time pre- Aryan invasion before the local forms of worship were marginalised in favour of the Vedic male gods in a priest oriented culture. These Aryan invaders were speakers of an Indo-European dialect, as were the Dorians who subjugated the Mediterranean, and the Phrygians who moved into Anatolia. In each of these cases a previously goddess worshipping culture is thought to have been suppressed and yet in each case the figure of the Goddess-head remains coherent. She is Ga and Rhea to the Greeks, Kybale to the Phrygians, and returns as the all-powerful Durga (who like Kybale rides on a beast, in her case a tiger) in the Puranic age in India. This coherency of Goddess-head has a direct relation to the equally long history and tradition of women sorcerers and indeed the whole feminine principal as being the sinister (from the Latin for left) and corrupting influence over man.

Greek Patriarchy and Women

In 1861 Bachofen, the Swiss anthropologist and sociologist, published *Mutterrecht* (Mother-right) which presented the radical view that aspects of pre-Aryan ancient Europe were matriarchal and that Mother Goddess worship was the prominent religion. He then proceeded to claim that the incoming patriarchal culture with its male gods was an 'evolutionary step' in the direction of greater consciousness, that goddess worship and all cythonic "mystery traditions" were of a lower evolutionary phase. Bachofen wrote in 1861, but the idea of women being lower on the evolutionary scale, of being closer to the old "madness" inducing Kybale type "Great Mothers", and thus retaining the power to corrupt or seduce the male, has indeed been prominent in Western European ideology since at least the time of the Aryan migrations. Since the Dorian invaders subjugated indigenous Mediterranean cultural traditions, the female has been marginalised and consigned to the realm of 'corrupter' in Western ideology.

To the Greek patriarchy, being antinomian meant being whatever the ruling male order thought was destructive to it, against it, or merely incomprehensible to it. Indeed, as Ruth Padel has noted, Greek patterns of fantasy reflect the ideology that women can threaten the male order and state of mind. According to Padel: "Most Greek Daemons, especially two classes, those which hunt human victims in groups (like Erinyes, 'Furies') or those which persecute the mind (again the Erinyes, or single demons such as Lyssa 'Madness'), are female. They are also cthonic (born of the Cthon, 'earth') and are sometimes described in phrases such as 'Daughters of Night'". She explains that "their femaleness is linked to their earth born status, their attack on the mind and their habitation in darkness. Fears of carnivorousness in female sexuality, underlying some of this material, are reflected in popular names for prostitutes like 'Lioness' or 'Panther'" (Padel 1993).

These aspects of the feminine, here literally demonised, feared or dreaded as an assault on male sanity and the sanctity of culture and law, found their counterparts in the Greek propensity for assigning to women ritual roles which pertain to these realms of darkness or material form, such as rites surrounding death and childbirth. In the Greek perception, women were considered to be more apt to deal with what could be considered 'polluting substances' such as corpses and blood in all forms including menstrual blood.To touch a menstruating woman or to enter a temple after intercourse with a woman, were forbidden acts and considered polluting to the male. The very nature of the feminine and the bodies of women were thought to contain polluting and corrupting substances.

In this perception, the female was "more likely to become possessed by a daemon" and contained a higher amount of the "black bile" or "melancholia" which darkens the *splanchna* ('entrails') (Padel 1993). It is in these organs of the *splanchna* which daemons are said to be able to easily infiltrate women. As the *splanchna*, which is the womb in a woman which is filled with the "Black Bile", it is vulnerable to possession by daemons; these daemons, it could be said, are the impregnators of the wombs, like a darker form of the God-rape so common in Greek myth.

Women and Witchcraft in Western Culture

We know that such perceptions of the female were retained in the Western culture into Roman, and Post-Roman Christian eras, reaching a crisis point during the witch trials of the late Middle Ages and early Renaissance. Among the accusations were having sexual intercourse with the Devil, attending the infernal sabbat and acts of black magic. The general idea of women, promoted by the main authorities of the inquisition, was that women were innately evil and allied to the devil. As the Malleus Malleficarum (Hammer of the Witches 1486) reads, "All wickedness is but little to the wickedness of a woman...What else is woman but a foe of friendship, an unescapable punishment, a necessary evil, a natural temptation, a desirable calamity, domestic danger, a delectable detriment, an evil nature painted with fair colours...Women are by nature the instruments of Satan--they are by nature carnal, a structural defect rooted in the original creation" (Summers 1928).

The prominent projection of women and/or the female principle as a poisoning element has been written about at length in modern times by traditonalist scholar Juilus Evola. Writing of the present Kali Yuga, thought to be a length of time (in Hindu aonics) of strife, war and destruction, Evola thought that Tantric acts which unite the male and the female transformed "poison into medicine". For Evola, the feminine principle is decadent and the primary force of what binds man to the earth and thereby, reincarnation; " it is a "truth"of non-Aryan races that are tellurgically and matriarchaly adjusted in outlook. Reincarnation...is conceivable only by one who feels himself to be a "son of the earth", who has no knowledge of trancending the natural order, bound as he is to a female-maternal divinity found alike in the pre-Aryan Mediteranian..and pre- Aryan Hindu World."(Evola 1996)

The dualistic negative-idealism implied in the Western perception of the female is comparable in its significance to modern moral dualist perceptions of the left or evil path of black magic articulated by Theosophy, which is responsible for much of the modern take on these concepts in the Western magical tradition. In the Theosophical view, the left hand path is both antinomian and anti-cosmic: it is contrary to both the social norm (Nomos) and the cosmic order, the God, making it both demonic and diabolical, indeed making the left hand path " black magic" (Blavatsky, Secret Doctrine, 1888)

Left-Hand Path Rituals for Women

For women on the Left Hand Path (LHP), the manifold traditional and historical perceptions of female sorcerers as evil seductresses or shrews who quarrel with their husbands and make pacts with the Devil may not be as insulting or as untruthful as they may have originally been. Rather, the LHP provides a female magician with the license to fulfil all her darkest feminist fantasies of dominance, demonic aggrandisement of the self and demonification of the feminine, independence and equality with the predominantly male demographic in modern sorcery, and a freedom from the mainly patriarchal morality of past eras. In effect, the LHP allows a woman to reclaim the thousands of years of male control over perceptions of her and to make use of negative images from the past for her greater power and wisdom.

In the context of modern sorcery, the Left Hand Path often includes communication with entities considered to be in direct opposition to the social morality of the day, including communication with various demons, especially those considered immoral by the Abrahamic religions. The ritual of the pact with the Devil, for instance, may be a communication with the very so called "dark forces" with which the western tradition has claimed her to have a natural attunement. In doing such a rite the female magician may be able to harness the power of the reality of such an attunement, as well as acting in a fashion which is in opposition to the social and religious conventions that threaten to suppress her.

Furthermore, the numerous strong female entities which are dealt with in the LHP are examples of how this aspect of modern sorcery made be used to further elements of a feminist agenda. Dark Goddesses and Demonesses are awakened not only as purveyors of an aeonic strategy to liberate the female in a repressive male order, but also in order to awaken the perceived feminine power of the practitioner. On the LHP this practice serves to bring forth the destructive and warlike qualities of the entities and reify the traditional 'polluting' aspects of female biology to the effect of creating both gnostic and sorcerous insights which may, again, be used to counter personal or political repression. This practice is in effect similar to the original practices mentioned above with regard to the Shakti; the feminine, though dark and cthonic, is still the sacred and holy impurity, as Ma Kali is met in pollution of the cremation ground for the gnosis of her midnight mysteries.

Lilith, originally a child-killing Sumerian demoness now often invoked on the Left-Hand Path, is an entity much maligned in Talmudic literature as a controversial figure who was Adam's first wife in the paradisiacal garden of Eden. She was so annoyed with his refusal to try a sexual position other than the missionary, that she flew away and met up with Samael, who was apparently more accommodating in that respect, and with whom she subsequently spawned a race of baby demons. The Lilith story demonstrates a Jewish vilification of the same female superior sexual position held to be supremely sacred in Vamamarga tantra, which is performed exclusively with the women in the superior position as opposed to the missionary. And, as Lilith is equally maligned in Kabbalistic texts, in which she is the demoness of the sphere of earth and considered a polluting and corrupting force, it is clear that the LHP practice of conjuring her is similar to the various Tantric practices of honoring the dark material aspect of the Shakti in the demonic feminine.

Lilith, who defies the mono-maniacal patriarch Yahweh and the prototype of the human race in Adam, is also the ideal example of the type of antinomianism said to be a quality of LHP practice in which the individual is liberated from servitude to Abrahamic religious doctrine and made to stand independent, powerful and self actualised. LHP practice could in this way be argued as being a fertile ground for the female sorcerer to release her traditionally "natural" antinomian and demonic powers for her greater personal fulfilment as well as an aeonic feminist strategy; as Lilith flies away from convention and glories in the power of her sex (literally), the female sorcerer may use the power of taboo breaking and feminine sexual energy to elaborate her own context as well as to alter the male order.

Prominent Women Satanists

The popularity of identification with the name and persona of "Lilith" amongst women of the Left-Hand Path and the gothic and vampire subcultures generally, was presaged by Lilith Aquino, *nee* Patricia Sinclair, founder of the Lilith Grotto of the Church of Satan in New York in 1971. Lilith Aquino became one of the founders of the Temple of Set after the secession of the majority of the Church of Satan's Priesthood in protest of the 1975 decision of its founder, Anton LaVey (Howard Stanton LaVey), to sell ordinations. Frequently interviewed, Lilith Aquino also became publicly known as a Grand Master of one of the Temple of Set's internal Orders, the Order of the Vampire.

The Temple of Set was also host to another prominent woman of the Left-Hand Path, Zeena Schreck, *nee* LaVey, daughter of Anton LaVey and Diane Hegarty. Ultimately rejecting the non-theistic Satanism of the Church, Zeena's membership in the Temple of Set ultimately resulted in schism, as her own understanding of the Left-Hand Path emphasized its tantric context to the exclusion of the transcendental individualism generally favored in the Temple. Following her 2002 election to – and departure from – the office of High Priestess, she and other like-minded former Setians formed the "Storm" which presented itself as the "vanguard" of the "International Setian Movement," emphasizing the significance of initiatory shock, erotic initiation, antinomian transgression, extremism, fanaticism, and religious conversion experiences as necessary mystical elements of Left-Hand Path liberation. Zeena's primary collaborator and magical partner, her husband Nicholas Schreck, co-authored with her a successful book concerning Left-Hand Path sexual magic, *Demons of the Flesh* (Schreck and Schreck 2002).

Similar applications of extreme antinomianism, fanaticism, eroticism, and transgression are found in the initiatory and magical practices of the Order of Nine Angles, a small sect in England. According to its own account this order allegedly continues an archaic, pre-historic indigenous tradition venerating a dark goddess later associated with Albion who is propitiated with the sacrifice of young men. According to Nicholas Goodrick-Clarke in *Black Sun*, "The modern history of the ONA began in the 1960s when [a] woman [leader] united three obscure neopagan temples called Camlad, the Noctulians and Temple of the Sun as a new order." (Goodrich-Clarke 2003). The Noctulians still exist as the esoteric core of the Temple of Blood, a similarly clandestine magical group in America, utilizing a similar magical and initiatory system combining practices of vampirism and the veneration of a variety of cthonic entities. The founder of the Society of the Dark Lily, also in England, was the noted Satanist Magda Graham, whose initiatory system bore close resemblance to that used in the Order of Nine Angles.

In contemporary times self-proclaimed Satanic priestess Diane Vera founded the "Church of Azazel," which focuses on the religious veneration of the Devil and demons. Maxine Dietrich, *nee* Andrea Harrington, founded "Joy of Satan Ministries," which combines literal religious devotion to Satan and demons. Harrington associates Satan with pre-Christian pagan divinities as the divine benefactors of humanity. She also encourages the Satanic equivalent of dualistic spiritual warfare against Abrahamic religions and their priesthoods.

The artistic dimension of magic is equally dramatically represented by Left-Hand Path women, including the famous Australian artist Rosaleen Norton, whose demonic images have been compared to the work of Austin Spare; Steffi Grant, wife and magical partner of Kenneth Grant (their works delve into the significance of Spare and the western application of the *Vama Marg*); and Linda Falorio, whose "Shadow Tarot," an exploration of the worlds of the "qlippoth," or "shells" of primordial, cthonic creation referenced in the Lurianic Qabalah, is heavily indebted to Grant's consideration of the theme in *Nightside of Eden* (Grant 1994). These diverse figures share a common identification with the primal, female, dark, cthonic, potentially destructive but creatively fertile current of the Left-Hand Path.

The Dark Goddess as Mother Goddess

Though dark Goddesses and demonesses may be called by the title of "Great Mother" such as Kybale or Durga or Kali might be, they are rarely actually depicted with children. Indeed, there they are an aspect of the feminine which embraces motherhood without embracing a child, or being specifically associated with a child. They are independent from their offspring, which refutes the Bachofen thesis that the reason why the Goddess worshipping culture was of a lower order of consciousness was because motherhood is common to all of nature whereas fatherhood is recognised only by mankind. In fact this is quite incorrect, for we know that penguins for instance have a high consciousness of fatherhood. The Mother Goddess as divorced from her offspring and the feminine principal liberated from childbirth but retaining motherhood could be seen as an evolutionary step in its own right, and one in the direction of an individuated consciousness. The female is emancipated from the physical but retains the spiritual or magical aspect allowing a primitive society to honour the feminine principal as divorced from the 'fertile, child bearing' image.

Since the modern version of the Left Hand Path is one of non-union and of individual consciousness, it would seem that the original "Mother Goddess" cults of dark goddesses such as Kybele might be the first occurrence of the human psyche in a state of non-union with the immediate physical. Indeed, in the tradition of the Shakta Tantras, when the Devi (shining one), having been created by all the gods to fight a great battle for control of the universe, is accused by her enemy of fighting unfairly because she receives the help of other fierce Goddesses (Durga, Kali, Chamuda, Ambika, ect) she makes an interesting claim. According to Elizabeth Harding: "I am all alone in the world here... these Goddesses are but my different powers. I stand alone". (Harding 1998)

Kali, as a goddess of death, directly opposes the child bearing image. As the mother goddess of death, she is the creatress of the first stage of the alchemical process, the mortificaltion and putrifaction, the death process of the psyche on the path to enlightenment. Stanton Marlan describes Kali this way in his book about the 'black sun' , the *Sol niger*. This death process is known in alchmey as a nessessary step on the path to *conjuctio*, the final illumination of opposites. (Marlan 2005). In the last stage of the alchemical process, in which the putrifaction continues thoughout, the individual is immortalised in an individuated Self , which in turn is conscious of its male and female qualities in a spiritualised chemical mariage. This is closer to Evola's concept of the female as earth bound (death bound) and cythonic, but is not maligned nor ignored. Rather in Western alchmey as in Indian Tantra, the female is considered without question the first and the last step to realisation and inidividuation of the enlightnened self and ego.

The Left-Hand Path in My Life

The **aeonic** power of a woman on the Left-Hand Path is that unlike modes of Western esoteric practice which are focused on male gods promoting purity and obedience, and in which the physical female is often seen as a demonic and impure force, such as in some of the variations of Kabbalistic tradition, here, the woman is able to reach equality with male practitioners, and her traditional darker aspects are glorified. On the Left Hand Path I am able to stand alone like Kali, without a male consort, without being either ignored or sexualised by men. Since the LHP is a path of non-union, I am able to detach from any element of repression directed at me by a patriarchal system, and to exist as an independent entity in the eyes of my fellow practitioners. On the LHP this much maligned feature of the female is able to come again into its greatest and most illuminating form; the **black** creatress who stands alone, who is alone, who is the one which greets you at the gates of the **midnight** sun on the cremation ground of all past repression, who is the very architect of freedom.

I have found the Left Hand Path to be a place of power in the patriarchal society in which we live, and have experienced working with the darker aspects of the Goddess-head to be in line with my personal goals and outlook. It is the independence of the demonesses and the non-child bearing aspects which suit my particular feminist strategy. It is certainly the case that among Left hand path practitioners and feminists such as myself such dark goddesses are invoked for the purposes of self- illumination. These invocations are what lead us to an aspect of the human mind that craves individuation. The decent into the body of the Goddess, or the decent of the Goddess into the Hades such as in the case of Persephone, is a intiation into the nature of the individual psyche and Self. This process of decent, the backwards path, in which we leave the rational and materialist world of daylight and pleasantry, is the real beginning of the work of the magician, a venture into the unknown of the personal and actual void. For when we decend, we do so with the sight we are capable of, and in the darkness we see the attracting and repulsing forms of the resplendant self. This is the realisation of the Skakti, the Kali who's darkness we take on, we become, we know inside and out, through which we can become the illuminated and immortal entity of the individuated Self. This is a teaching of profound individuality, for the old Goddesses are themselves without consort, without child, without the traditonal attachments of the female, proving that to honnor her is to honnor the death of the weak, suffering and repressed self and to usher in an new personal aeon of the Goddess-head of the Self, the incarnation of the Goddess in the personality of the witch.

Is it also perhaps that the decent into Hades and the mating with the devil in a male form may be the equivalent of the male-driven tantric practices? It is well known that though Skakti is worshipped in Tantra, it is difficult for a woman to get intiated into the practice herself. Tantra is a cult of men worshipping women in order to perfect a form of sexual alchemy in which they may become free of the oposition. Why not then, should the cult of women worshipping the male cythonic principal in the form of Satan or the Devil, be considered more radical? Satanism as a devil worshing cult in the modern age may be womanhood's answer to Indian Tantra, a sexual alchemical work with the male equivalent of the Kali or Dark Mother. It is a cult of the Dark Father, the Father of Lies,with whom the woman can mate as the Dark Goddess, just as the Tantric initiate invokes Shiva to mate with Kali. Through this work, the women may rise to spiritual heigts more prominent than their male allies, at least within the Satanic circle, in the same way that male *Tantrikas* dominate the Tantra in the East. This is a possible "female path" for the Western woman; the decent into the darkness of the self, there to meet with the devilish opposer who's seed one must consume in order to awaken the male in the self, and therein to unite the opposits in the individuated mind. More work needs to be done on such subjects and the way is hopefully opening for that dialogue to take place.

To conclude I would like to share the following aeonic evocation of the Dark Goddess in the traditional style of Satanic inversion of the Lords Prayer:

ALU

Our Dark Mothers of Malingned and Blasphemous Name, (Who are Lilith, Kali, Sekmet, Erishkigal, Astarte, Babalon and more) HAGAL
Who Dwell, our Sisters, in the Earth, (Who are Kybale, Durga, Hekate, Persephone, Innana and more) URDA
Hallowed be your ancient names (Which are Ka, Ba, Hekat, Lilitu, Isis, Taltos, Rihannon, Morgan, Tiamat, Hel, Druj and more) KEN
Your Aeon Come, (Which is the Aeon of the Black Sun, the Hel-Gap and the Vulva) EOL
Our Will be done On Earth, This Time, This Place, DAGAZ
Give Us this Day our Ultimate Knowlegde, Gnosis and Independance, GEFU
Our Pleasures, Our Rewards, Our Indulgences and our Satisfactions. ING
Grant Us Abundance of Victory. SIGILA
Forgive not those who tresspass on our bodies, our works or our freedoms, and let us not forgive those who trespass your names, habitations and occupations. THURSIS
Lead us always into temptation to aquire greater power, greater knowledge and absolute self soverenty, ANSUS

Women and the Left Hand Path

And deliver us from weakness, from ignorance , from death and from rebirth, MANAZ
For Ours is the Aeon, the Power and the Glory, the Individuation and the Immortalisation, TIWAZ
For Ever and Ever, ODAL; IZA; RAHU

AO.

References

Alesha, Matomah (2004). *First Book of the Dark Goddess: A Study and Reflection on the Primordial Dark Mother,*Tucson, Ariz.: Matam Press.

Aquino, Michael A. (1983, 2009). *The Church of Satan, Sixth Edition* San Francisco, California.

Bachofen, Johann Jakob (1861). *Das Mutterrecht:eine Untersuchung ueber die Gynaikokratie der alten Welt nach ihrer religioesen und rechtlichen Natur mit Untersuchungen von Harald Fuchs,Gustav Meyer und Karl Schefold.* Basel: B.Schabe, 1948

Blavatsky, Helena (1888). The Secret Doctrine: The Synthesis of Science Religion and Philosophy. Sacred Texts: www. Sacredtexts.com. Last accessed 31.7.09.

Coward, Rosalind (1983). *Patriarchal Precedents: Sexuality and Social Relations,* London, Melbourn, Boston: Routledge.

Evola, Julius (1996). *The Doctrin of Awakening: The Attainment of Self-Mastery According to the Earliest Buddhist Texts.*Rochester, Vermont: Inner Traditions.

Flowers, Stephen E. (1997). *Lords of the Left-Hand Path: A History of Spiritual Dissent,* Second Edition Smithville, Texas: Runa-Raven Press.

Goodrick-Clarke, Nicholas (2003). *Black Sun: Aryan Cults, Esoteric Nazism and the Politics of Identity* London: New York University Press.

Grant, Kenneth (1994). *Nightside of Eden,* London: Skoob Books Publishing.

Harding, Elizabeth U. (1998). *Kali: The Black Goddess of Dakshineswar,* Delhi: Motilal Banarsiddass.

Hixon, Lex (1994). *Mother of the Universe: Visions of the Goddess and Tantric Hymns of Enlightenment.* Wheaton, Ill.: Quest Books.

Marlan, Stanton (2005). *The Black Sun: The Alchemy and the Art of Darkness.* USA: Texas A & M University Press.

Michaels, Mark A. and Patricia Johnson (2006). *Essence of Tantric Sexuality*, Woodbury, Minn.: Llewellyn Publications

Padel, Ruth (1993). "Women: Models for Possession by Greek Daemons." *Images of Women in Antiquity*, Avril Cameron and Amelie Kuhrt, eds. London: Routledge.

Patai, Raphael. (1990). *The Hebrew Goddess*, Detroit: Wayne State University Press.

Schreck, Nikolas and Zeena (2002). *Demons of the Flesh: The Complete Guide to Left-Hand Path Sex Magic*. England: Creation Books.

Summers, Montague (1928). *Malleus Maleficarum (1486)*, (online), accessed 6/1/09. http://www.sacred-texts.com/pag/mm.

van Lysebeth, Andre (2002). *Tantra: The Cult of the Feminine*. Delhi: Motilal Banarsidass.

Yates, F. (1979). *The Occult Philosophy in the Elizabethan Age*. London and New York: Routledge.

Biography

Sybil Black is a traditional witch, ritual-theatre artist, and demonologist. A natural antinomian, she first conjured the Devil at the age of six. A priestess of Satan and Hekate and a fire-witch on Loki's side, she is also a founding member several occult orders including the Esoteric Order of the Black Sun, Cultus Viae Nocturnum and the Temple of the Devil. She lives in Europe where she has continued to study the implication of Gnosticism and Traditionalism in the Black Arts.

LILITH, BABALON, AND SEXUALITY

The stereotype women magicians most often face is that of the sexually available partner of male magicians. In this section women confront the magical category "female passive, male active" to reframe women's sexuality in their own terms.

    Alison More reviews the history of Lilith as the Biblical woman who rejects Adam's demand for her sexual submission. Kirsten Brown traces her own relationship with Lilith as the woman who stands alone and with Babalon as the woman who chooses her relationship with others. Leni Hester draws on the imagery of the sacred prostitute that was one of the sources of the biblical Babalon to create ritual expressing her own sexuality. Finally, Lupa directly confronts sexual dimorphism to create non-polarized sex magic through the vehicle of kink sexuality.

THE ROSE OF SHARON OR A THORN AMONG LILIES: LILITH IN MYTH, TRADITION, AND CULTURE
ALISON MORE

You gotta give it to Lilith
she was a hell of a woman
Said she'd rather
fuck demons on the beach
than lie under the belly
of that whiner Adam
& flew from Paradise
(Maison, 1992)

In the modern psyche, conflicting images of Lilith endure. She is the dark goddess: the choice between submitting to patriarchal rule and unending exile was clear. Unhesitatingly, she claimed herself and fled. She is sexual power. She has no need of men, and in her freedom she subverts the gendered paradigms which are otherwise firmly entrenched in western thought. She is the dark feminine. She embodies those aspects of the psyche that we are afraid to touch. She is the destroyer. She renews the face of the earth. In the twenty-first century, the traditional images of Lilith as demon, harlot and destroyer are empowering. However, this woman, goddess, or demoness is, in many ways, as mysterious as the darkness she represents.

The diverse and conflicting images of Lilith are a gift to psychoanalysis, academia, Jewish feminism, feminism more generally, modern paganism, and ritual magic; however, it is important to realize that they are not entirely the product of modern imagination. Throughout her four-thousand year career, Lilith's powers have been perceived as divine, diabolical or occupying a liminal place between the two. The roots of her image or images originate in ancient Babylon, but are shaped into a cohesive image only in medieval Jewish texts. The Lilith who today is a feminist archetype, and the Lilith who was a demonic archetype in the

Middle Ages was shaped by a tale recorded in the *Alphabet of Ben Sirach*.

> "After God created Adam, who was alone, He said, *'It is not good for man to be alone'* (Gen. 2:18). He then created a woman for Adam, from the earth, as He had created Adam himself, and called her Lilith. Adam and Lilith began to fight. She said, 'I will not lie below,' and he said, 'I will not lie beneath you, but only on top. For you are fit only to be in the bottom position, while am to be in the superior one.' Lilith responded, 'We are equal to each other inasmuch as we were both created from the earth.' But they would not listen to one another. When Lilith saw this, she pronounced the Ineffable Name and flew away into the air. Adam stood in prayer before his Creator: 'Sovereign of the universe!' he said, 'the woman you gave me has run away.' At once, the Holy One, blessed be He, sent these three angels to bring her back.
>
> "Said the Holy One to Adam, 'If she agrees to come back, fine. If not she must permit one hundred of her children to die every day.' The angels left God and pursued Lilith, whom they overtook in the midst of the sea, in the mighty waters wherein the Egyptians were destined to drown. They told her God's word, but she did not wish to return. The angels said, 'We shall drown you in the sea' (Baskin 2002).

To modern feminists this text is attractive as it shows a woman who fought against the establishment of the patriarchy from its earliest days (Daly 1990). Although desiring equality brought Lilith only banishment, her acknowledgement of herself as Adam's equal, and the rejection of this by the Divine validated the institutional rejection internalized by many first-wave feminists.

Although there is some mystery surrounding the author of the text, this is undoubtedly not his intention. The unknown author of the *Alphabet* is often assumed to be the anonymous author of Ecclesiastes, but is regarded as something of a parody in some Jewish scholarly circles (Stern 2004). The dating of the *Alphabet* is equally uncertain: it was written somewhere between the eighth and tenth centuries. Certain scholars have found textual evidence suggesting that this story may have been circulated orally in earlier centuries, but nothing conclusive exists (Patai 1964).

Roots: Babylonian

So who was Lilith? Certainly a female being, or beings, by this name first appeared in a tablet bearing the story of *Gilgamesh and the Huluppu Tree*, dating from approximately 2000 BCE (Kramer 1939). The tablet tells the tale of a tree the goddess Innana planted in her sanctuary, and planned to use the wood to furnish her home. She was thwarted in her plans by both a dragon and Lilith, the "maid of desolation," making their home at the base of the tree along with the Zu-bird and its young. Witnessing Innana's heartbreak at her lost tree, Gilgamesh is spurred to heroism and slays the dragon, causing the Zu bird to take flight with its young, and the heartbroken Lilith to flee into the desert (Patai 1964).

This tale says nothing of Lilith seeking retribution for her unceremonious eviction; however, it is not long before other texts begin to speak of Lilith's vengeance. In the abovementioned Babylonian tale, she causes a goddess associated with childbirth to experience both distress and disruption within her domestic sphere. When her hatred for domesticity is considered in conjunction with her title of "maid of desolation" and her associations with both evil and a serpent, the later image of Lilith, the demoness with a particular hatred for pregnant women and children, the dark feminine and the creatrix of disorder, does not seem an illogical development. Nevertheless, this was not her only guise in Babylon. A terracotta relief portrays Lilith in her winged magnificence carrying a rod and ring (Patai 1964). In this relief, Lilith is no longer demonic, but divine. As we will see, both the pantheons and mythologies of the ancient and medieval world were resplendent with Lilith the demoness, Lilith the goddess, and combinations thereof.

Roots: Biblical

Lilith has the dubious honor of being demonized by at least four major religious traditions. In addition to her Babylonian heritage, she appears in the Judeo-Christian scriptures. The book of Isaiah reads: *Wildcats shall meet with hyenas, goat-demons shall call to each other; there too Lilith shall repose, and find a place to rest.* (Isaiah 34:14

The Rose of Sharon or the Thorn of Lily

New Revised Standard) Lilith is not mentioned by name in all translations of the bible. Her name is often replaced with terms such as "night hag" or "screech owl" (Waldman 2008). In the Latin Vulgate, her name is replaced by *Lamia*. Rather than simply a translation of Lilith, the appellation Lamia emphasizes the destructive aspects of Lilith's legend. Lamia had the misfortune of being impregnated by Zeus, and tricked by his jealous wife into murdering her own children. She was considered a figure of feminine evil throughout the Middle Ages (Leinweber 1994).

The child-killing associations are also seen in the seemingly innocuous substitutions for her name. The epithet "screech owl", or *strix, strigis* in Latin became the modern Italian *streghe*. In modern Italian, *streghe* is a standard word for witch, but in the later Middle Ages the term had a more specific meaning. The *streghe* were a type of witch, known for breaking into homes at night to drink the blood of infants, which bears a startling resemblance to the Lilith mythology (Kieckhefer 2006).

Another tradition portrays Lilith as a jealous spirit. Angry with Adam for allowing her to be banished, the demoness seduced her former husband in his sleep. Her intent does not seem to have been mere seduction, but rather the conception of offspring which resemble their mother in her hatred of the human race. Although this tradition is not developed until the *Zohar* of the eleventh century, Lilith and her demonic offspring (the *Liliu*) were objects of hatred and fear in the ancient world.

The Isaiah passage illustrates that the demonic and chaotic associations of Lilith persisted into the Jewish culture of the eighth century BCE. As further evidence of Lilith's career as a Jewish-demoness, biblical archeologists have uncovered skulls from the same period. Believed to originate from Jewish communities, these skulls bore Aramaic inscriptions either invoking curses or protecting the bearer from the same curses. A number of these skulls refer to "Lilith" and the "Liliu" (Levene 2009).

The majority of magical fragments bearing the name of Lilith applied to childbearing. A number of fragments enticed or commanded Lilith to stay away from either women during the final stages of pregnancy or their newly-born children (Levene 2009, Patai 1964).

Solomonic Legend

Through marriage, Lilith added to her growing collection of faces. A Greek manuscript, *The Testament of Solomon,* relates another face of Lilith. This text relates that Solomon was in possession of a magic ring through which he could command demons. Though there are other legends in which he could "make the *Lilin* dance", the *Testament* recounts Solomon's meeting with a demoness who challenged him directly. This spirit with a woman's head and no limbs, claimed that "though you have sealed me round with the ring of God, you have done nothing." She explained herself, saying, "You will not be able to command me. For I have no work other than the destruction of children." (Klein 2000).

As is the case for many strands of Lilith's story, the version of Lilith being conquered by a human king is neither the only nor the dominant version of Lilith's encounter with Solomon. Instead, she became associated with the Se'irim, or hairy demons. In these tales, her upper body was unbelievably - yet deceptively - beautiful, while her true nature was revealed by her beast-like hairy legs (Waldman 2008). Through adopting the guise of feminine beauty she could lure men to their damnation.

The *Zohar* relates a different version of Lilith's marriage - while the slave of Solomon, she was first of the four demonic wives of Samael- his queen, and therefore queen of the realm of evil. In a direct reversal of the heavenly court, Lilith was seen as the mother of the damned (Waldman 2008). As is discussed later, this image recurs again in Renaissance texts.

Lilith in the Middle Ages

Lilith's career as composite demoness continued throughout the Middle Ages. Based on the legend of Lilith's seduction of Adam, Lilith-demons became succubi, that is, demons in the guise of beautiful women whose evil inclinations caused a preoccupation with non-reproductive sex (Elliott 1998). Like the Babylonian Lilith, her sisters the succubi subverted the natural order of the family. Succubi tempted men to sexual fantasies which culminated in either nocturnal emissions or demonic offspring (Boyarin 1995). Although her influence was felt in the Christian west during the Middle Ages, the medieval Lilith was a composite figure. Fragments of her demonic past - her ability to destroy homes, marriages, and both her hatred of and need for children - combined to create a female entity who was feared but not fully understood.

Demons, as fallen angels, had no physical bodies, and no fixed sex. Of course, this would render the myths of demon children, and tales of women impregnated by demons virtually nonsensical. As both were fairly common motifs in various genres of medieval literature, another explanation was required. No less a thinker than the Dominican Doctor of the Church, Thomas Aquinas, theorized that,

> "...occasionally an offspring is born from copulation with a devil. In such cases, the semen would not come from the devil himself, properly speaking, nor from the body he had assumed, it would be from the seed of men taken for the purpose; and the same devil would receive it from a man and impart it to a woman..." (Summa Theologica 2006).

Demonic offspring were somewhat problematic. As they hated children, succubi and demonesses or *Liliu* would have had no interest in children for their own sake. Instead, these offspring were portrayed as demonic, intent on destroying the human race through subversion of the natural order. Succubi would not necessarily perform sexual intercourse with their male victims; tempting thoughts culminating in nocturnal emissions would serve equally well for propagating the demonic brood.

As composite demoness, the medieval Lilith acquired new legends throughout the Middle Ages. The legend in the *Zohar* of Lilith as the queen of the damned became a virtual mirror of the cult of the medieval Queen of Heaven, the Virgin Mary. Lilith is often portrayed as the mother of Lucifer. In a direct parody of a *topos* associated with the Virgin Mary, Lilith sings her son's praises in the diabolic courts. As Jeffrey Burton Russell points out, "in Hell, as on earth, the role of the female [was] to honour and admire the male" (Russell 1992, Waldman 2001).

It is difficult to say whether medieval Jewish texts presented a more favourable picture of Lilith than their Christian counterparts. It is true that the threads of her story which could be seen in Torah and Talmud were brought together in the *Alphabet of Ben Sirach*; however, while this tale is seen as empowering by feminists in the twenty-first century, the images it uses are not necessarily flattering to women. For all his possible affinity with the genre of parody (Stern 2004), the anonymous author of the *Alphabet* presented the model of a woman who was disobedient to her husband, and banished from paradise as a result.

Renaissance and Early Modern Periods

Part of the Lilith-legend that is difficult to date is her knowledge of the Divine name. Legend states that after her expulsion from Paradise, Lilith dared to approach the heavenly throne. After seducing and deceiving the Most High, Lilith wrested from him the most secret of secrets and fled to the caverns by the Red Sea (Waldman 2008). Although there is no textual tradition for this, the legend has persisted in occult circles, and was particularly emphasized in Renaissance Hermeticism.

Renaissance Hermeticism emphasized the role of the erotic as "the outcome of a mystical nostalgia for the disappearance of God" (Waldman 2001). The idea of the negativity in mysticism was popular throughout the Middle Ages. Renaissance Hermeticism attempted to give concrete voice to this tradition. In particular, the attraction of the feminine was particularly attractive to those associated with the Hermetic tradition. The feminine associations of Jewish mysticism, in particular Kabbalah, ensured that it remained a powerful influence in western esotericism. The symbols of Jewish mysticism were both concrete and explicit, and at the same time implied a dualism which could easily be translated into Hermetic terms. Both spoke to the need for balance between masculine and feminine, and both acknowledged the four elements earth, air, fire and water as the four primordial elements.

The association of Hermeticism and Jewish mysticism made it both natural and logical that the hermetic role of divine feminine, the wife and wisdom of God, was ascribed to Lilith. Versions of the end of Lilith's marriage to Adam changed again. Adam, created in the image of God, was right to assert his dominance over Lilith who was not. After her expulsion from Paradise, Lilith gained her own control, through the abovementioned ploy of discovering and uttering the Divine Name.

In the eighteenth century, an edition and translation of a twelfth-century invocation protecting children was published. Attributed to Elzear of Worms, this charm directly invoked "the second Eve" and asked that she neither harm women in childbirth, nor the infants they bore (Klein 2000). The powers of charms and amulets which protected women against harm persisted throughout the eighteenth century, particularly in traditional Jewish circles.

Although Lilith did emerge as a powerful figure in hermetic and occult circles, it was as much because of her negative associations as in spite of them. The figure of Lilith emerges as the dark consort of the light masculine principle. Even her overtly demonic associations with seduction and the destruction of family remained: in Aleister Crowley's *De Arte Magica,* Adam begat the race of demons with his demon-lover Lilith (Crowley 1987).

The Modern Lilith

The dark goddess or beautiful demoness was a tragic figure: wronged by both man and god, she carried tragic scars which could only find expression in gruesome revenge. The oscillating faces of beauty and evil, or the goddess and demoness captured the hearts and imagination of artists and poets. Lilith and her sisters Circe, Melusina, and Lamia, emerged from realms of religion and mythology to the world of art and literature. Men such as Goethe, Rossetti and Keats found a dark muse for their art or writing in Lilith's dark feminine archetype (Scerba 1999). In particular, Rossetti had an almost visionary influence of the modern feminist interpretation of Lilith: he emphasized her reluctance to be subservient to Adam, and styled her as a virago - an image that had increased her appeal to modern feminists.

In the late 1990s, the Canadian foundress of the festival "Lilith fair" described the legendary goddess or demoness as follows:

> Adam...asked God to send him a mate, a partner like the other creatures had. God obliged by making Lilith and sending her to Adam. At first he was pleased, but then she opened her mouth, showing that she had a mind of her own. He wanted her to lie beneath him and she promptly refused, saying that they were equal and she would not be subservient to him. Adam flew into a tantrum, so Lilith took off to calmer territory (McLachlin 1998).

The details are not dissimilar to the version in the *Alphabet of Ben Sirach*, but the interpretation is very different. Both the blatant sexual conflict and the subsequent choice to wander among demons are conspicuously absent. More recently, the Jewish feminist theologian, Judith Plaskow, has published works completed throughout her career in a volume entitled *The Coming of Lilith* (Plaskow 2005). Rather than being limited to Jewish, or even Jewish - Christian dialogue, the issues raised by these papers touched feminist writers and theologians from all religious traditions and none. In a response to the reaction to these papers, Plaskow stated that the issues raised in these collected works allowed diverse women to transcend division and focus on what united rather than what divided (Plaskow 2007). Reclaiming and re-interpreting the Lilith-story is common in modern feminist circles, academically, spiritually, and psychologically. In magical circles where the community is diverse, but women are a minority, this can be even more important.

Conclusion

It is important to keep in mind that conceptions of Lilith have neither been universal nor static. Instead, from her earliest incarnations as both demoness and goddess, to her modern roles as both an alternative to patriarchy and the feminine side of the psyche, perceptions of Lilith have been in constant oscillation between cultural conceptions of magic, the demonic, and the feminine. Lilith's identity is neither fixed nor stable. However, the complex and composite identity which makes it difficult, if not impossible to find the real Lilith, has another side: ineffability renders the dark goddess accessible. As with any complex individual, it is easy for the modern practitioner of magic, scholar, writer, artist, or feminist to find useful and appealing threads in the Lilith-legend. Following each strand of her story will lead to a deeper understanding of this representation of the dark goddess.

References

Aquinas, Thomas. *Summa Theologia: Angels.* (2006). Kemelm Foster (Tr.) Cambridge: Cambridge University Press.
Baskin, J. R. (2002). *Midrashic women: formations of the feminine in rabbinic literature.* Harvard: Brandeis University Press.
Boyarin, D. (1995). *Carnal Israel: Reading Sex in Talmudic Culture.* Berkeley: University of California Press.

Crowley, A. (1987). *De Arte Magica.* Sequim, WA: Holmes Publishing Group.
Daly, Mary. (1999). *Gyn/Ecology: The Metaethics of Radical Feminism.* Boston: The Beacon Press.
Elliott, D. (1998). *Fallen Bodies: Pollution, Sexuality, and Demonology in the Middle Ages.* Philadelphia: University of Pennsylvania Press.
Kieckhefer, R. (2006). "Mythologies of Witchcraft in the Fifteenth Century." *Magic, Ritual, and Witchcraft, 7,* 79-108.
Klein, M. (2000). *A Time to be Born: Customs and Folklore of Jewish Birth.* Philadelphia: Jewish Publications Society.
Kramer, S. N. (1939). *Gilgamesh and the Huppulu Tree.* Chicago: University of Chicago Press.
Levene, D. (2009). "Rare Magic Inscription on Human Skull" *Biblical Archaeology Review,* 35, 46.
Maison, J. (1992) "One Hell of a Woman" [poem]. In D. George, *Mysteries of the Darkmoon* San Francisco: HarperOne Press.
McLachlin, S. (1998). Introduction. In B. Childerhose (Ed.), *From Lilith to Lilith Fair* St. Martin's Griffith Press.
Patai, R. (1964). Lilith. *The Journal of American Folklore,* 77, 295-314.
Plaskow, J. (2005). *The Coming of Lilith: Essays on Feminism, Judaism, and Sexual Ethics, 1972-2003.* Boston: Beacon Press.
Plaskow, J. (2007) The Coming if Lilith: A Response. *Journal for Feminist Studies in Religion,* 34-41.
Russell, J. B. (1992). *The Prince of Darkness: Radical Evil and the Power of Good in History.* Ithaca: Cornell University Press.
Scerba, A. (1999). *Changing Representations of Lilith and the Evolution of a Mythical Heroine.* Pittsburgh: Carnagie Mellon.
Stern, D. (2004). The Alphabet of Ben Sira and the early History of Parody in Jewish Literature. In James L. Kugel & Hindy Najman (Eds.), *The idea of biblical interpretation: essays in honor of James L. Kugel* (pp. 423-47) Leiden: Brill.
Waldman, F. (2001). Jewish Influences in Medieval European Esotericism. *Studia Hebraica,* 86-98.
Waldman, F. (2008). "Local and Universal Folklore: The Story of Lilith." *Studia Hebraica,* 96-107.

Alison More is a social and cultural historian of religious movements. She has earned a doctoral degree in medieval studies. She currently resides in New York State. Though she works primarily on feminine forms of religious expression that emerged during the high Middle Ages, she maintains an enduring interest in the changing face of the feminine in various religious traditions.

EVERY TIME YOU PLAY THE RED, THE BLACK IS COMING UP
KIRSTEN BROWN

I seem to be drawn in everything I do to things that tend towards being boys' clubs. Art and illustration in particular, technology and computers, those were longstanding and understood from the get-go, but I didn't expect it when I grew bored by what the various avenues of Neopaganism had to offer me, and began to explore chaos magic. I'm not going to go into the social mores that still annoy the hell out of me, the oneupmanship and 'wand'-measuring contests, but rather into some of my own experiences. I only provide this for a bit of where I'm coming from. Some of the hardass reputation might have helped draw me to it, but I was intrigued more by the what-works-for-you nature of it than anything else. I could piece things together, experiment without being told by books and peers that I was 'doing it wrong'.

Lilith was one of the first deities I explored in the framework I began building for myself around these ideas, and the only goddess I really felt anything from or towards. I started out working with her likely due to the reasons you always hear from young women stepping into this kind of thing; the feminism bit, the transgression, the bad-girl-from-the-Bible bit. I've always gotten on better with guys and the gods are no exception, but there was something there. A relationship in which I began as a child and a student, or somewhere between the two.

Like all relationships, things grew more nuanced. Nearly from the beginning, Lilith began to teach me not to fear the unknown, though I'm a poor student in some areas and I still get my ass handed to me for it. I learned much more about her by exploring other things I was drawn to, like primal serpent energies and fallen angels. Following threads outward and tying it all together. I learned a lot about her different faces through anger, because for a long time I was afraid of anger. My way of dealing with it up until then had been simply to cry. Then I found myself in a mentally and emotionally abusive relationship, and I reveled in the power that anger could bring when I no longer felt I had anything to lose. When I finally realised that my own reactions were making him cling more, I learned how to let go of it and then him. Without really looking back, I moved seven hundred miles away to learn what a healthy relationship was like.

I knew about Babalon. I remember trying to read the Bible as a kid, and only ever making it through the Revelation. I remember woodcuts and paintings from Europe and the Puritans in history and art books, and seeing her there, astride the Beast. When I started my magical study and came across her again, I wasn't much impressed. Here was cosmic tits and ass, something for the Crowleyites to stick their wands in, to justify sticking their "wands" into everything they could while pointing at her and saying "Look! We're not sexist!" Another thing for women involved in magic to feel they had to live up to, another Goddess defined by who they fuck. I have been deeply dissatisfied with the archetypes offered for women in most magical practice for a while, especially since I came to a conclusion that in working with them, we take on traits of them in how we connect with the Universe, and this just added to my disappointment.

Reading Alan Moore's *Promethea* was possibly the first step in softening me to her a bit, in showing me that there was maybe more to her than a celestial pinup. The power of his depiction, as well as interaction with women involved with her current, people working deeply with it whom I respect and now call friends. I was intrigued enough to pick up a book that was being reprinted last summer, about her and about the author's experiences with her. It was a relation of devotional work, which I have a fascination with. I read it, processed it, though I still saw nothing of myself in there. I am not a bombshell, a seductress. I don't use my 'feminine wiles' to get things, and have never been comfortable with the idea of doing so. I'm something of a tomboy who wouldn't know if someone found me attractive if I was hit with a brick that proclaimed so. I take care with my appearance so that self-consciousness isn't an issue, because it's more mentally and emotionally efficient that way. But the curiosity opened a door, and there was a red-stockinged and high-heeled foot keeping it from closing. Looking back, maybe the influence had begun with the itch to have the book in the first place.

Before going to sleep some nights, I try to go Up and Out, descriptors I prefer to calling it 'astral'; sometimes it takes me places before I pass out. It's like meditation and daydreaming and writing stories I don't wholly control. In June or July of 2008, I did this and found myself on a grey stone path, up the side of a mountain. It was windy and darkly cloudy there, and I entered a cave, opened a door.

Every Time You Play the Red, the Black is Coming Up

Lilith was there, in what looked like a small apartment, complete with a stove, a bed, and a big black dog; she'd taken the face of a tall older woman with long black dreads and sharp, dark eyes, more human than the Giger-esque being I usually see. I don't remember what passed between us anymore, other than that I was given a lantern and quickly ushered out the door, down another path to an iron gate entwined with roses, brambles, with the feeling of being dropped off at an aunt's house. I understood what was happening, somewhat, but not why or the extent of what was to come. I resented it, because my initial response was to wonder if I was going to have to start wearing lipstick or miniskirts or something.

Things began to come along in waking life, lessons that connected with my new ideas of what Babs was, with very little of the subtlety I was used to in dealing with the nonphysical. It wasn't the usual chains of pointing synchronicity, though that happened as well. Opportunities for exploring my own personal and sexual limits and preferences presented themselves out of nowhere, involving people I trust to a good extent but never expected this from. I didn't follow on them, but following through wasn't the point. It was that I was approaching it, thinking about more than the ideals put across in porn and other media that I'd only recently became comfortable with, not reflexively accepting or refusing because I felt I should or had to, but considering clearly the patterns of possibilities and consequences.

August became something of an impromptu month of working. The month was bookended by eclipses, which led to a lot of synchronicity involving the Black Sun, a title for a personal avatar/embodiment of chaos I've worked with for years. I meditated on the Abyss and specifically the transition between the front and back of the Tree. I meditated on Her name as that which confines, or in my experience *defines* the gate as well as the key, by being the anchor that keeps you from losing yourself.

Between October and November, someone I'd done some work for came to me with an offer to draw an entire comic script. I hesitated. It was for an erotica anthology, and the theme of the comic itself was based around fellatio. It's one of the more uncomfortable acts for me - in that bad relationship it was something that was often forced on me, through guilt, manipulation and expectation, demeaning, bukakke, choking, all used to exert control. I accepted the graphic novella job anyway, needing the money badly and wanting the learning experience of doing a comic more than I didn't want to be confronted with these things. I'd worked with the writer before, and had been happy with the interaction, and I knew that part wasn't going to be something easy to find elsewhere.

At the time, I wasn't thinking much about anything deeper than getting this done, figuring out the intricacies of a whole new way of doing art, of how to take the script I was given, which was very freeform, and dividing it up. I found myself inserting elements of Babalon into the main character, an ancient sorceress looking to become young forever by trapping a djinn. Her younger self was only semi-consciously based on a drawing I'd done years ago of the Scarlet Woman and the Beast, and her summoning circles all had seven points. It wasn't until I got to the actual acts that I didn't want to draw, didn't want to face on some level, that all of this dawned on me, the purpose, the pushing, the subconscious dedication of the whole thing as a work in itself. I began to use it to exorcise the shame, the hate, the recurring bad feelings, by reducing the act as I reduce everything I do while I'm drawing it, to something technical, to shapes and shadows, then to something simply being done. A portrayal. In my mind, I could then begin to look at it more objectively, without the bad memories and associations. Each consecutive time I had to draw it, it was easier, and more of the old poison was filtered away.

Lilith taught me that subverting the Other, supposedly mastering it or driving it off, is not the answer, but results in suppression and repression, only making for twisted resentment and poisoned emotions. That taking it into one's bed, into oneself, knowing it, respecting it and maybe allowing it to change you and becoming stronger for it, is the lesson. That being hated for what one is can mean being feared, and in that fear is strength.

Babalon is teaching me that being free from shame is very different from being shameless. I am beginning to understand better where my limits lay, and that I really didn't ever have to be ashamed of being interested in women as well as men, or feel bad about *not* wanting to be naked at parties where shirtless-o-clock had been declared, or guilty for not wanting to be involved in anything I was invited to. My limits are *my* limits, to be pushed and tested on my own terms. I shouldn't fear sexuality, my own or others', but I should despise and avoid those that use it the wrong way.

Somewhere between reading Alan Moore's interpretation of Babalon, *The Red Goddess*, and working on the comic, in which the main character learns that her ultimate objective indeed comes with a price, I have been becoming more comfortable with the idea of being paid for my work, of compensation in general. If you want something, if it's worthwhile, you generally pay for it. I am learning that even the basest of whores receive payment for what they do, and I deserve to be paid for work whether it is my art or something else, and whether I am paid in money or trade, in respect or something else.

Babalon is showing me that I was becoming one-sided as a person as well as a woman, in working with little more than angels and Lovecraftian beings, and unconsciously trying my damnedest not to bring gender into the thing for all that sex, love, ecstasy and all their nuances are bound up with magic in many ways. That the antinomian and the transcendent require some balancing and grounding in the sensual and experiential, when you still have to interact with humans.

Between them both I've figured out that Woman in magic is not always, or even primarily, the receptacle and the passive force, nor does she have to be. Sometimes she is the crucible that burns away the detrimental and the unnecessary.

Biography

Kirsten Brown is an illustrator, visionary artist and semi-solitary chaote of about seven years (with time off for good behaviour) living near Atlanta, GA with her boyfriend and magical partner of five years, a household of varied other pagans, three cats, one neurotic shaven Collie, a garden and a ridiculous number of books. Along with her exploration of the power of art and story as both magical tools and workings in themselves, the Universe seems to have decreed it her life's work to make friends with anything and everything generally seen as Bad For You and Your Sanity, the latest installment of which was a surprise introduction to and subsequent devotional work with Lovecraft's Nyarlathotep and Azathoth via Kenneth Grant and a whole lot of Jagermeister on New Year's 09'. This is her first published essay.

WHORE: FREE YOUR ASS AND YOUR MIND WILL FOLLOW
LENI HESTER

Whore: Free Your Ass and Your Mind Will Follow
For I am the first and the last.
I am the honored one and the scorned one.
I am the whore and the holy one.
I am the wife and the virgin.
I am <the mother> and the daughter.
I am the members of my mother.
I am the barren one
and many are her sons.
I am she whose wedding is great,
and I have not taken a husband…
…I am the silence that is incomprehensible
and the idea whose remembrance is frequent.
I am the voice whose sound is manifold
and the word whose appearance is multiple.
I am the utterance of my name.
The Thunder, Perfect Mind
 (translated by George W. McRae)

The Qadesha (Qadishtu, pl.) were "one of a class of sacred prostitutes found throughout the ancient Middle East, especially in the worship of the fertility goddess Astarte (Ashtoreth). Prostitutes, who often played an important part in official temple worship, could be either male or female" (qedesha 2009). This term has come into usage by a new generation of priest/esses of sacred sexuality. In the ancient Middle East, the Qadishtu served such Goddesses as Innana, Ishtar and Astarte; Lilith appears in Innana's hymn as a ritual attendant long before she makes an appearance in the Old Testament.
    Very little is known about the function the Qadishtu performed within the temple, beyond a purely sexual one. They may have been a priestly class of performers, the musicians, poets and dancers charged with producing large religious festivals for large crowds several times a year. They may have been healers or

soothsayers. The archetype of the Qadesha is as much a modern construction as it is an ancient one. In our time it has come to mean magickal practitioners who draw upon an array of psycho-erotic practices from disparate traditions that frame conscious sexuality as a spiritual praxis. Inara de Luna, modern-day Qadesha and founder of the Temple of the Red Lotus, writes on the Temple's website: "The Qadishtu path and tradition are at once both brand-new and incredibly ancient. We are inspired by the original temple priestesses of ancient Sumer, who have been referred to by archaeologists as 'sacred prostitutes'. However, we have very little concrete knowledge today about what their priesthood entailed. We are left with vague references to their existence and activities, and many of these have been (possibly erroneously) interpreted for us by culturally biased researchers" (deLuna nd). The contemporary resurgence of the Qadesha archetype often manifests in a recognition of this energetic current in the lives of the individual practitioner.

The Qadesha is called forward to heal the grievous wound in the psyche caused by our culture's sex negative paradigm. Our toxic sexual culture, being rife with violence and abuse, injures all of us, regardless of gender and orientation. The Qadesha's sacred purpose is to offer the sacrament of sexuality as a vehicle for renewal, healing, and integration. Modern Qadishtu are able to draw upon a variety of body-mind technologies to affect this transformation. Yoga, ecstatic dance, drumming, Tantric and Taoist sexuality, fasting, massage, ritual, meditation, deep psychology, gender theory, ecopsychology, body modification, BDSM—all of these practices inform the Qadesha's service and deepen hir healing skills.

In recent decades, a resurgent interest in sacred sexuality has brought the Sacred Prostitute back into consciousness. Much has been written on this archetype as both a spiritual and political construct. I gratefully acknowledge the work of Annie Sprinkle, Cosi Fabian and MacKenzie Zeiss on this topic, and point my readers to their work to deepen their understanding. However important the theoretical and historical underpinnings of this trope are, my primary purpose in this essay is to discuss my experiences in consciously working with this current magickally. In these endeavors I was graced with a good deal of personal gnosis through my Guides and Deities. These are some of the moments of grace revealed to me, which have strengthened my connection to the Source, and which have supported my healing and the healing of my partners.

Leni Hester

Reclaiming the Sacred Whore

Awakening to my identity as a Witch meant reclaiming the word Witch. This is a common trope in Goddess worship: the reclaiming of words that are used as insults or trivializations in the dominant culture, becoming aware of the way words are used and misused to marginalize and dehumanize certain groups and individuals. A Witch was a powerful woman, free as no other women are, and vilifying her fearlessness, her shame-lessness, was obviously part and parcel of the dominant culture's need to marginalize what it feared, and to construct monstrous Others upon which to project its own ugliness. By the time I was embracing my identity as a Witch, circa 1990, the word had already been reclaimed and "rehabilitated" by the Women's Movement of the 1960s and 1970s. Moreover, concurrent with the second wave of feminist activism, new media images were depicting a positive vision of the Witch as young, hip, and glamorous. While this new Witch archetype represented rebellion from the dominant paradigm, her more fearsome and chthonian aspects were reassuringly softened. Invoking the power of the Witch into myself was an empowering and exciting thing, but it was not the act of audacity and courage it would have been for women of previous generations.

Much more dangerous was reclaiming another five-letter word denoting a woman outlaw, a woman beyond the pale of "respectable" society. This word was "Whore," and for me it was far more frightening.

In many ways I had spent my whole life in fear. Fear of what would happen, of what might happen, of what might not happen. The world, I was lectured, was a dangerous place, and only by hiding away from it and all its sources of danger, could I remain safe. Every step out into the world, away from the controlled shelter of my home, put me at risk. In adolescence this generalized fear solidified in the perils of high school politics. It didn't take long for me to become familiar with the scariest threat of my peers, among whom reputation is everything. For a girl, there could be no more crushing humiliation, no worse penalty than to be called a "whore." Once this name was stuck to you, you could not get free of it. Once branded a whore—and there was no actual criteria for earning this epithet, and the motives of the person who leveled it like an accusation were never examined—you lost all credibility. Your word was never sufficient, your abilities at any task were questioned, you were ostracized. In any argument, your opponent

Whore

could call you out and the debate was over—there was nothing more to say, you just lost.

The hostility and contempt with which "whores" were treated at my school was shocking to me, and I resolved never to be branded with this word. My efforts were in vain because by age 12, despite being a childish, unattractive virgin, I had been labeled a "whore." I was not exactly sure how that happened back then, but eventually I came to understand the power of such a word as a tool of control was a symptom of a dominant paradigm that was at its heart deeply misogynist. It wasn't until much later, after becoming a Witch, that I was able to reclaim the word Whore as an aspect of my psyche, as a powerful source of gnosis with my Matron Goddess and as the core of my magickal work.

The Rite of Liberation

This ritual was performed on March 20, 2007, to capitalize on the energies of balance at the Equinox and the deep soul knowledge of a Dark Moon. Informed by Qabalistic magick and Transformational Craft, the stated intent here was to integrate and balance two contrary forces in my psychosexual makeup. On the one hand, I acknowledged my tendency to become unbalanced and co-dependent in my sexual relationships, which manifests as a feeling of enslavement to the relationship. At the other extreme, I was acknowledging my tendency to react violently against the feeling of being trapped, and to run from confining relationships with explosions and drama, often obliterating relationships with my lover and friends, burning bridges with my associates in order to achieve "freedom." Both of these tendencies have negatively impacted my life, and taken together they indicate to me a lack of conscious decision making and balance that doesn't serve my autonomy, sovereignty or my ability to love appropriately.

I framed these two tendencies as the iteration of the Western body-mind split as it manifests for me. Although I don't generally play with polar binaries (good/evil, man/woman, light/dark) in ritual context, I really did recognize my own divided, ambivalent process at work here. It could be couched in terms of the perennial Madonna/whore split, but recognizing both of these behaviors as points of a continuum encouraged me to employ the Qabalistic Pillars, the Pillars of Severity and Mercy, to hold these energies. The Middle Pillar, between the slave and the escape artist, was the Qadesha, the one who can hold the balance of the two within herself and therefore can heal and be healed. Coming to this center point of balance was the intent of the ritual, but as items and revelations about both my enslaved and liberating selves piled up, I knew that moving to center would take some work.

The left side of the altar was raw black silk, with a black Hecate doll and her spinning wheel and a black candle. In front of this were my black leather and chrome wrist restraints. On the right, on top of white linen, was a small statue of Our Lady of Mercy, known in Santeria as Ochanla (the female aspect of Obatala). Ochanla is pertinent here because in her Catholic iconography she is shown holding manacles in one hand, belying her function as a liberator (She liberates sinners from their sins). Next to this were a white candle and the key to my restraints. In the center was an amber colored candle for the Qadesha, and a black & white cookie.

In prepping for this ritual I recalled moments of being enslaved and disempowered by sex, times when I gave my power away to a lover or a rival, times when my sexuality was injured and when it made me vulnerable. I had to acknowledge the ways in which I colluded with my disempowerment. I recalled the moments when I was strong and self-protective in relationship, when I pulled the plug on unhealthy ones against much pressure and resistance. I acknowledged in that the heady rush of liberating myself, I made poor choices, I manifested unconscious dramas and compelled people I cared about to be part of them, I burned bridges with allies and friends in a frenzied rush to "liberate" myself from my own bad decisions. Holding these two energies, I felt myself moving slowly towards balance, able to be in service but also to maintain strong boundaries and sovereignty. I had to acknowledge the benefits that each had brought me, and accept them into myself before I could move into that desired place of strength and balance at the center.

I created sacred space with water and salt, flame and tears of myrrh. I called in the elemental Guardians at the cardinal points, and grounded into the red iron of the Earth with a four-fold aligning breath and a modified Cosmic Cross. I stood to the left and addressed my enslaved self. Putting on the restraints, I lit the black candle and gave thanks to her for all she taught me, for all the ways she had served me, and to release her from carrying that burden anymore. I felt a release at this moment, several muscles in my back relaxing gently. I felt as if something had returned to me. Moving to the right, I lit the white candle and picked up the key to my restraints. I addressed my liberating self, thanking her for all she taught me and all the ways she had served me, releasing her from that burden. Here I didn't feel a release but the air to my right became cooler and fresher, as if a window had opened.

At the center, I held each energetic in my out stretched hands. Toning "om" I brought the two together over the Qadesha candle and into my core. Lighting the center candle I addressed the Qadesha as the resolution of these two forces. I thanked Her for all she taught me, and all the ways She had served my highest good. I thanked Her for the opportunities She presented for me to heal myself, and pledged myself for carrying this work forward in the world. I performed the Middle Pillar to anchor and integrate the work into myself. And then I ate the cookie, to further anchor this change on the physical plane and to provide a cue of sweetness, pleasure and comfort to this integrating step.

Neurochemical Manipulation

There is a moment about ten seconds or so after orgasm, when the flood of dopamine released by the climax hits my blood stream. Regardless of whether the orgasm itself was mild or powerful, the dopamine rush is always intense, hitting my whole body with an almost unbearable sweetness as it makes me stop, catch my breath, feel my knees get weak. Before I became aware of this chemical harbinger of the famous "afterglow", I could be walking, perhaps to the bathroom, or getting dressed, or trying to move back into the other activities of my day. My knees would buckle, my head would reel, my stomach would hurt, and I'd feel thrown off center. Now I quietly wait for it, and when the hormonal tide hits my cells, and each nerve begins to sing with the piercing pleasure of it, I lean back and ride the crushing waves of physical ecstasy. If it's dark I can close my eyes and watch my capillaries pulse and sparkle with this substance, and I lose myself in its beauty. Already laid out by my orgasm, the chemical blowback of the dopamine flows into the rivers of my fluid body—my blood, my interstitial fluid, my cerebrospinal fluid—and I can feel my body on a cellular level reveling in a grace that feels holier than prayer.

In this moment I receive flashes of the past and future, I have insights into things I have never ever dreamed of, the faces of my Gods are revealed to me, their voices reach me and I hear them loud and clear. I have profoundly vivid moments of personal gnosis, revelations couched in metaphors that are perfectly clears to me, but so deeply personal that I could never explain them to anyone. I take this opportunity to do some metaprogramming of my psyche in this exquisite moment of "imprint vulnerability." I will give myself an affirmation, or set up keys of memory so that I can integrate this moment of gnosis into my "walking around" life. If I'm working with a sigil I will project the power of this energy right into it. Changing consciousness through will is a Witch's business, and with the power of the orgasm to propel my will, I call for wholeness and healing. I call for the love of the Goddess to wash over me in exquisite waves of delight. I call on myself to receive this blessing despite a life time of sex-negative programming and experience. I offer thanks and praises for the Qadesha, the Sacred Prostitute, the Holy Whore whose archetype manifests in various guises and spiritual currents, the one who has known me, and loved me, and taken me for Her own.

References

McRae, George, tr (nd) *The Thunder, Perfect Mind*. Retrieved (May 16, 2009). The Nag Hammadi Library. Web site: http://www.gnosis.org/naghamm/thunder.html
qedesha. (2009). In *Encyclopædia Britannica*. Retrieved June (May 16, 2009), from Encyclopædia Britannica Online: http://www.britannica.com/EBchecked/topic/485699/qedesha
de Luna (nd). Temple of the Red Lotus (nd). Retrieved (May 16, 2009). Web site: http://www.templeredlotus.com/

Biography

Leni Hester is a Witch, writer, ritualist and artist living in the Denver area with her husband and two young daughters. A priestess of Ochun, a devotee of the Blessed Virgin, and a practitioner of Transformational Witchcraft, she unites decades of occult study in the Western Mystery tradition, Wicca (Alexandrian and Gardnerian lines), Lukumi, sacred dance and yoga to create a powerful, multivalent spiritual praxis she has named Arbor Vitae witchcraft. She was a ritualist and Handmaiden for the Lunatic Fringe (North Carolina, 1991 to 1996), and has since been working on co-creating powerful, multicultural ritual experiences in various magickal communities. Leni has been a regular contributor to SageWoman, New Witch, and Pangaia magazines, and her work has appeared in *Manifesting Prosperity* and *Pop Culture Grimoire*, both from Megalithica Press.

THE FEMALE KINK MAGICIAN
LUPA

Note: While much of the descriptive language I will be using in this essay focuses more on cisgender women — that is, women who were born in bodies with XX chromosomes — most of the material in this essay is equally valid for transgender women. Additionally, my experiences as a cisgender woman necessarily color the writing to an extent. In no way should this be taken as a suggestion that the essay is meant only for cisgender women.

Sex magic has historically been a male-dominated field, at least in Western occultism. For the most part, women have been relegated to passive roles in sex magic; oftentimes the woman isn't even required to be a magician herself. Much of this can be attributed to rote adherence to heterosexist polarity, in which the male is the "active, quickening" element, and the woman is the "passive, receptive" element — nothing more than a glorified cum receptacle.

BDSM-flavored sex magic tends to be more egalitarian between the sexes (or among, if you take the wonderfully pansexual view that there are more than two binary sexes). While male-dominated D/s (Dominance/submission) relationships are more common, it's understood by most kinky people that female-dominated relationships — and non-heterosexual ones as well — are every bit as legitimate. Many of the people writing about kinky sex magic are either actively non-normative when it comes to sex and/or gender, or openly support people who are in their writing; Raven Kaldera and others who write about the Ordeal Path are a good example, and my husband Taylor and I did our absolute best to be gender- and sex-neutral in writing our book *Kink Magic: Sex Magic Beyond Vanilla*.

While it's not impossible for the modern vanilla female sex magician to act on an even level with her male counterparts, with kink sex magic there's not a long history of active suppression of the female element as anything other than passive, and a strong thread of fucking (no pun intended) with hidebound stereotypes. Therefore there are several ways in which kink sex magic can be utilized by the female sex magician to diversify her roles in sex magic; even the vanilla sex magician may find inspiration for her own practices.

Destroying the Myth of Polarity

The first step in breaking female sex magicians out of the strictly passive role is to shatter the overly dualistic view of sex and gender that for too long has dominated sex magic (and, to an extent, western occultism in general).

At first glance, it would seem obvious that duality is only natural. After all, most of the species of animal, and many plants, that humans interact with on a daily basis are sexually dimorphic. Humans, too, largely fall into the biological categories of "male" or "female". This tendency towards focusing on dualities has spread to more abstract concepts, such as "good" and "evil", and caused us to assign subjective values to seemingly binary phenomena such as "day" and "night". Oftentimes, in our attempts to create meaning through cosmology, we connect these pairs in ways that seem logical to us. Therefore in some interpretations of Christian mythos, "woman" is "evil" because she is the one who accepted the fruit from the snake, and therefore "man", being "good", is to be the head of the household as he is more trustworthy (though still answerable to YHWH, it would seem).

However, biologically and individually speaking, asexual and hermaphroditic beings outnumber sexually dimorphic ones overall. Humans tend to be anthropocentric, and so focus more on beings that resemble us the most; hence the popularity of animal totems as opposed to plant totems, and the most popular animal totems being, unsurprisingly, mammals. No wonder, then, that even with the increasing amount of biological knowledge we have at hand, we still characterize "nature" in sexually dimorphic terms. Even characterizing all humans as sexually dimorphic is a mistake. Aside from intersexed people who were born with primary sex characteristics of both sexes, some transgender and other gender non-normative people openly embrace sex as well as gender identities that are neither (or both) male or female.

Some people try to excuse dualistic approaches to sex magic through the concept of physical fertility. Yes, sexual fluids are central to most sex magic practices. However, does this mean that magicians who are unable to procreate can't have effective sex magic? Considering that all of the magic referenced in *Kink Magic* was done while I was unable to have children, I'd have to disagree strongly. Additionally, much of sex magic relies on energy carried by sexual fluids, not the fluid themselves (unless someone has discovered how to alchemically change semen into physical gold).

The Female Kink Magician

Biological sex aside, gender roles have become increasingly flexible in the past few decades in the West. While there have always been women willing to buck the system, it's much more acceptable for women to work outside the home, have masculine haircuts and wear pants, delay having children (or not have them at all), and otherwise break out of the feminine/housewife role. While the shattering of male gender roles has been slower to catch on, it's more acceptable for men to express emotions, particularly vulnerable ones such as sadness, as well as be primary caretakers of children than it used to be. Unfortunately, there's still work to do, to include in magic. While neopagan religions tend to be heavily female-oriented, Western occultism is still largely the domain of men, and female magicians may still find themselves marginalized or objectified.

Another important consideration is that not everyone is heterosexual. There are magicians (generally, though not exclusively, male) who insist that sex magic must involve one man and one woman in order to work correctly; this can include everything from the Wiccan Great Rite to "purple magic" in Chaos magic. This may sound good on paper to those who make these claims, but they fail to address numerous acts of successful sex magic performed by same-sex couples (or groups!), or that otherwise don't follow along the heterosexist stereotype.

Therefore, the woman is not automatically locked into the passive role. What else, then, is available to her?

The Woman as Active Principle

As men have largely been the writers of recent history, that history has been highly biased. Even the way we describe things can be highly gendered. Let's look at the active/passive duality in sex magic for a moment. The man, because he is the possessor of Tab A, which is then inserted into Slot B, and emits semen (which at some points in history was believed to be the only element necessary to creating a baby; once again, women were nothing more than convenient receptacle).

Yet let's try writing that a different way. Imagine, if you will, a woman on top of a man — cowboy or reverse cowboy will do. As she wraps her legs around him, holding him in place, she immerses and engulfs him within her vagina[1], possessing him within herself. She then stimulates him to give up an orgasm, and draws forth his semen, which she captures and keeps. She has taken power from him.

See how different that is from the more common language of a man "thrusting", "nailing", "pounding", "entering" and otherwise acting upon a largely passive woman? She may "rise to meet him", but there's still the suggestion that she only re-acts to him. This sort of language goes hand in hand (or penis in vagina?) with man-on-top missionary, which necessarily has the man as the active principle. And while there's nothing wrong with that in and of itself, we're here to discuss the woman as the active principle.

The main problem is that women continue to be valued primarily for their reproductive qualities. If you look at most sex magic, the part of the woman's anatomy that's most important is her vagina—the hole that the male magician sticks his amazing magical cock into. Very few sex magic texts ever talk much about the woman's clitoris, or the differences between the clitoral and vaginal orgasm. Like a bad romance novel, any mention of a woman's orgasm is assumed to arise from stimulation from coitus.

However, the clitoris is directly analogous to the penis. In fact, they stem from the same bit of fetal tissue, changed primarily by hormones in the womb and thereafter. It's probably not too much of a stretch to equate the female clitoral orgasm with the male penile orgasm. Any woman who's had a clitoral orgasm (and yes, there are those who have not) knows just how much energy is *expended* when it happens. Isn't this a projective, active force? And, just as with the male orgasm, with practice the female orgasm—whether clitoral or vaginal—can be focused and directed for a magical purpose.

This means that a human being need not have a penis in order to be the active principle (and, in some cases of pre-op MTF transgender people, possessing a penis need not even automatically mean identifying as male). There is, of course, the option of strap-ons, for either the dominant or the submissive (again, reminding the reader that a phallic object, fleshy or otherwise, doesn't automatically mean "in control"). However, these are absolutely not

---

[1] Just as a side note, the terms "vagina" and "vulva" are commonly confused. The vagina is specifically the opening and shaft of a woman's sexual anatomy, whereas the vulva is a term for the more general female genital region, to include the mons, both sets of labia and the clitoris.

necessary whatsoever, and may be used or discarded at your preference.

The Mechanics of the Thing

So how, exactly, does non-polarized sex magic work? Well, how does magic in general work? In order to break out of your previous assumptions about a particular topic, sometimes it's advisable to go back to the basics of it. In this case, you need to think about how you believe magic works.

Let's use energy as an example. Here, magic is believed to be the result of manipulating a form of energy that may not be detectable by modern scientific methods, but which exists nonetheless, permeating the entire universe. Energy is passed between/among the participants in sex, in magic, and pretty much any other interaction. Sex magic is the act of manipulating that energy using sexual activities for consciously directed magical purposes.

Now, where in that does it say that you have to have a man and a woman for it to work? It doesn't. All that's needed is energy; anything beyond that is personal, subjective preference. Unfortunately, most of the writers on sex magic have shoved their own preferences so thoroughly into their material that they've convinced entirely too many readers that what's subjective is actually objective[2].

So let's look at the basic energy work of sex magic a little closer. You need at least two participants. Generally speaking these are going to be two adult human beings. However, a solitary sex magician may also utilize evocation of spirits/imagination/etc. to gain a willing partner in the absence of a consenting human partner. And for some forms of sex magic (such as the wank-and-fire method of sigil casting), all you need is yourself and some self-lovin'. However, for the purposes of kink magic, let's assume at least two consenting, fully informed adult human participants[3].

---

[2] If you aren't already well-versed in sex magic, a good non-dogmatic approach may be found in Brandy Williams' *Ecstatic Ritual*. Please see the reference list at the end of the essay for further recommendations.

[3] I have occasionally run across sex magicians who didn't inform their partners— who may or may not have been magicians themselves— that they were doing sex magic. I find this to be highly distasteful; ethical magic requires consent just as ethical sex does. Considering magical practice can harm someone even if they

There are a couple of ways to work with the energy. The way that may seem most intuitively matched to kink is with one person directing and the other person receiving—the active/passive roles. Again, there's absolutely no sex or gender based standard here, and as I'll explain in a bit the dominant need not even be the active magician! The other method is for both participants to be active principles in magic, working in tandem. While this may seem tougher to achieve in a situation where power exchange may be enacted, it is possible.

I'll discuss specifics of these two currents of energy work with regards to the two main general roles in BDSM (and, of course, kink magic).

The Female Dominant Magician
In some ways, it's easier for the dominant to be the primary magical practitioner in a kink magic ritual. She has the control of the ritual (scene), and can decide what needs to happen, when, and how. Here are a few ideas for starters:

--Using the submissive as a magical battery: All that wonderful energy that the submissive is creating in response to all the various things the dominant is doing to her is a great source of energy for magical practice. A dominant with some experience in energy work[4] can easily siphon off as much of that energy as she likes to put towards the purpose at hand. This can be done at any and all points within a ritual, up to and including sex (though this is not absolutely necessary).
--Using the submissive's body as a magical tool in physical ways: Whether cutting, leaving trails of wax, or carefully applied impact play, the dominant can create sigils and other magical symbols on the submissive's skin which can then be charged with the energy of the ritual.
--Shamanic Pony Play: Ever heard how the shaman's drum may be referred to as a "horse"? Let the submissive be the horse instead. While the rhythm of flogging and other impact play is well-known

---

aren't consciously aware it's going on, it's in everyone's best interests to be honest.
[4] If you have never worked with energy work, you'll probably want to have a basic understanding of it before trying something like using someone else's energy. For Western energy work, *Hands of Light* by Barbara Ann Brennan is a good choice; B.K. Frantzis' *Relaxing Into Your Being* is a nice primer on Eastern, specifically Taoist, energy work.

for putting the submissive into a trance, the dominant acting as a shaman may use that same rhythm from the other end to go into trance herself. In this case, it's crucial that the submissive not trance along with her, as once the flogging/etc. is done it will be the submissive's duty to watch over the dominant's body while her spirit flies.

The Female Submissive Magician
On the other hand, it's easier in other ways for the submissive to be the main magical practitioner in a kink magic ritual.

--Sensory overload/deprivation: These are good choices for submissives who have some experience with altered states of consciousness[5]. While the dominant may be doing the work in bringing the submissive into the altered state, the submissive is the active magician in using that altered state to make the magic occur. This can be anything from a shamanic journey to divination to sigil casting.
--At Your Command: In some cases, the submissive may be a more skilled magician than the dominant (or the dominant may simply not feel like doing the magic herself). In this case, the dominant may direct the submissive to work magic on the dominant's behalf. This may be done in a ritual together, or the submissive may be ordered to do it on her own time.

Either/Or, and Working Together
--Invocation: This takes roleplay to an entirely different level! Instead of merely pretending to be entities, the magicians may actively call the entities into themselves at some preappointed point of the ritual. This can be deities, spirits, or other noncorporeal beings; it may also be different "selves" of the magician, or even general archetypes.
--Evocation: In evocation, a magician calls an entity forth, but not into herself. The entity may be called forth into the general ritual area. However, the magicians may also evoke the entity into her partner; this differs from invocation in that the person receiving the entity is not the one actively calling the entity forth. The dominant, for example, may wish to use the submissive as a vessel for evocation. Conversely, the submissive may call forth a terrifying or

---

[5] If you're not experienced in altered states of consciousness, I would recommend Diana Paxson's *Trance-portation* as a wonderfully thorough primer.

otherwise powerful entity using her respect or other feelings for the dominant.
--Working magic together: Two (or more) magicians may work magic together. This is commonly seen in magical groups. How the magicians synchronize the magic is up to them; they may do the same action together, focus on the same goal at the same point in the ritual, or even enact a particular ritual psychodrama (which may or may not involve invocation/evocation).

A Note on Switches

Taylor and I developed our interpretation of BDSM sex magic as switches. We personally find that switching opens up a lot more opportunities both for the individual magician, and everyone involved in a relationship in which kink magic may be utilized. Obviously, not everyone is a switch (though we encourage people to at least give the other side a try, if for no other reason than to make absolutely sure. That, and we adore needling the people who claim that "switches don't exist".). So if you're a switch, feel free to partake of any and all of the ideas above, and run with them. Otherwise, use what works for you, and perhaps find someone willing to take the other side.

Kink Magic and Feminism

It's my hope that this more egalitarian view of sex magic has given readers some good ideas for breaking sex magic—kinky or vanilla—out of the male-dominated sphere, and into "anything goes!" territory. Kink in general is subversive (as is magic), even if not all of its practitioners see it as such. Culturally, at least in the United States, while occasional media references pop up, the general view is that it's still taboo.

Sadly, in some people's minds (including in the U.S.) the idea of assertive, powerful women is also taboo. The modern occult community is not immune to this bias. Even if the sexism is subtle, it's still there, whether in the form of "old boy's" clubs in lodges, or in women's voices being silenced time and again. While neopaganism has many strong female voices that are acknowledged and seen on an equal par with men, female occultists often feel we have to shout to be heard.

With kink magic, traditional gender roles are thrown out the window. Women are free to be dominant (or willingly submissive—

or switchy), as are men. "Male" and "female" are not the only choices for sex and gender identities. Heterosexuality is not seen as the only or even the best option for everyone. And women aren't seen as lesser than men; my experiences in the kink community in general, and BDSM sex magic practitioners in specific, I've been in safe space for the most part, something I can't say in my everyday life.

Of course, even being a dominant woman doesn't make one immune to objectification. Numerous female doms can attest to having dealt with (generally male) submissives who came into a D/s arrangement with a long laundry list of expectations and fantasies which essentially reduced the dominant to a warm female body with a flogger. Still, the various subversive elements in kink, magic, and the combination thereof make this a useful tool for shattering mainstream, often outdated, paradigms, and introducing more flexible, healthy ones.

References

Dawn, Crystal and Flowers, Stephen (2001). *Carnal alchemy: A sado-magical exploration of pleasure, pain and self-transformation.* Smithville, Texas: Runa-Raven Press.
Easton, Dossie and Hardy, Janet W. (2004). *Radical ecstasy: SM journeys to transcendence.* Oakland: Greenery Press.
Ellwood, Taylor, and Lupa (2007). *Kink magic: Sex magic beyond vanilla.* Stafford: Immanion Press/Megalithica Books.
Hunter, Jennifer (2004). *Rites of pleasure: Sexuality in wicca and neopaganism.* New York: Citadel.
Kaldera, Raven, et.al. (2006). *Dark moon rising: Pagan bdsm and the ordeal path.* Massachusetts: Asphodel Press.
Williams, Brandy (2008). *Ecstatic ritual: Practical Sex Magic.* Stafford: Immanion Press/Megalithica Books.

Biography

Lupa is a neopagan and (neo)shaman living in Portland, OR with her husband Taylor Ellwood, their two kitties, and more than enough books and art supplies. She is an avid gardener, hiker, sustainability geek, and grad student. She is also the author/editor of several books/anthologies on pagan and magical topics. She may be found at:
http://www.thegreenwolf.com

http://therioshamanism.com
http://paganbookreviews.com.

CULTURE BEARERS

To be a culture bearer means to carry a language, art, memory or history, regional or racial identity, from one generation forward to the next. Women often end up in the position of culture bearers as women often end up teaching the next generation, both in the home and in the classroom.

Some forms of magic only pass in this way, quietly from the hands of women preserving them to the people who surround them. This magic is intimate and private, discussed only within the trusted core of the family or community. The magic itself is bound up in the movements of daily life, focusing on the everyday needs of the people who work that magic, the needs of caretakers, gardeners, cooks, lovers, to keep household, family and community intact.

Teresa Garcia talks about the magic she has learned from her family and the magical world around her. Byron Ballard speaks as an Appalachian woman preserving her community's traditions. Kris Leet muses on the experience of inheriting traditions in need of preservation and repair.

The voices in this section are the ones that are easiest to overlook, the quiet voices that do not contest the ground of conversation when they are spoken over. To hear these voices we must make the space for them to speak, sit quietly, and listen.

WORDS SPOKEN BENEATH THE WILLOW
TERESA GARCIA

My Magic

Magic is a large part of my life, and has been since I was very young. It was as a two year old that I met my guardian. As a child I began to learn about healing by observing my mother. I read about magic and religions both while growing up, even though a great deal of what was available in the books I had access to sounded rather biased against magic. It never made sense to me when most of my peers would say that magic wasn't real. As a child, I knew magic was real. I saw it. I saw the glow around new leaves and could feel the soft flow as "something" moved through everything.

What my magic hinges around is personal transformation and care of the family, striving and reaching to be the best that I can. I do the best I can with my family, and when I cook for them I focus on the magic of enhancing health and enjoyment. My workings have been known to involve protection of loved ones, both within my biological family and my spiritual family. I paint or draw to share visions and ideas. I write stories to both entertain and to give things to think on, to cause people to wonder "what if" and to take a short break from their busy lives. I have done healing work in the course of being a mother, daughter, and friend. I have been at the side of a dying person, the very man that helped to give me bodily life. With my mother, we helped my father to let go and rejoin the ancestors when his battle with cancer drew to an end at home. I have seen the border several times because of my work in the magic of life, and my own brushes with the chance to pass from one state to another. The mere act of living and loving, to me, is magic, and to live well is Deep Magic.

I must add, I am still learning the Deep Magic, and always will be. Whenever I learn something, I find more that must be learned and applied. It is a cyclical process, at least for me. I have not figured out if this cyclical nature is what drew me, or if it resulted in the way that my mind now functions, or some combination of both. I often feel as if I live in more than one world and must be a bridge between the two. I've been told this many times and in many ways.

Magic, at least the way I've learned to do it, is very personal. Through the cycle of the month, due to how my body feels, my activeness in magic and my personal energy waxes and wanes. During my menstruation I become very still energetically. A great deal of that is from my cycles being particularly painful all my life, so I always thought of it as a protective mechanism. I focus on things that I can get rid of at this time, since I also get aggressive. At this time, for me, protective spells and charms also seem to be more potent than if cast at other times, which I sometimes think could be attributed to my tendency to push most everything and everyone away at this point. During the rest of my cycle, emphasis is put on encouraging projects to mature.

I have no name anymore for my magical path, since it is so much part of my everyday life, and it is separate from my religious path to some extent despite how all parts of my life overlap. For the record, my religious path is best currently described as an unnamed blend of Shinto and Wicca focusing on Sun, Moon, Storm, Mountain, and Sea. Though I am not of Japanese descent, studying Shinto has helped me understand my guardian's viewpoints more.

If pressed for a name for my magical practice itself, I'd have to label it a family tradition in that much of what we do as a group is things learned in childhood from other family members. This has been augmented in some areas we found lacking. My mother and I have both been learning about what other people do and about our heritages, and incorporating some of those practices. It has also been interesting to come across things that we knew of intuitively and to have confirmation of these things. Therefore, when working individually we are eclectic as well. I've heard the term Hedge Witch, and that somewhat fits, but I really hesitate to use that and prefer to just go about what I do and not bother with labels too much. Too many labels can fit, but not fit "just right."

As my guardian once said "You'd get along just fine without a name, a name only comes into play when somebody needs to talk to you, and sometimes not even then. Your energy is your name, really, and that is why eventually you won't bother with one for what you do, *because* you won't be able to utter it with your mouth or write it with your hands. You will only be able to act when it is time, and when you reach that point, you'll have remembered a great deal." I should add that he followed that statement with the fact that I'll also have forgotten quite a bit too.

Teresa Garcia

Magical Practice

I usually only speak details of my practices with a few individuals, so speaking even this frankly feels strange to me. Some of these individuals my personal practices are involved with, others I am not involved with as working partners, but these people have opinions I value greatly. I sometimes, every once in a great while, speak publicly on my personal blog.

Trying to talk to Grandma about the things I saw when young was how I first learned to be careful who I talked to about what. Though my mom was open to talking to me about things, her mother-in-law seemed to be afraid when I would point out the fairy in her garden when we'd visit. When I was old enough for school, it wasn't fear that I encountered, but ridicule because, "trees don't talk, angels and fairies aren't real, and dragons are fairy tales." One classmate, who became a very good friend and still is today, believed me though. That was all I needed at that time, to be believed by someone other than my mother, and so I pressed on in figuring out how energy worked, my steps into the world of magic. Many years later, I learned that "silence" was part of the Witches' Pyramid.

There are some times that I find silence hard to maintain though. I am rather distrustful of people in general, but I would like to trust individuals. Talking to the wrong person or at the wrong time has sometimes made my practices more difficult, at least in the short term. Talking to my father as I grew, though at first it hampered them, in the long run actually made them easier as I had outside input and he grew to trust my judgment. I did not get to discuss all of my practices with him, but when the topic would come up, it was beneficial because I knew that he wanted to be certain of what I was doing and my safety.

An interest of mine, from my childhood over twenty years ago, is working magic with dragons. My first memory of working with them, at least for this life, was when I was two and wandering my grandmother's yard. That is when I met my guardian, who I didn't know was called a dragon until I was older. I never thought to ask him directly what he was, it didn't matter to me. I just knew that I liked how he felt and that he cared about what happened to me. In our ensuing talks together I felt like I understood a bit more about the world and how it worked. He often helped me by explaining how things that I saw going on worked. I learned early that the energy of a dragon felt very different from that of a tree, or a garden fairy, or the angel that I sometimes encountered near Grandma.

When I wasn't interacting with adults, I was interacting with nature. I had a tendency to sneak outside or go for walks when everyone was busy. On hindsight, I think that part of why I met my guardian so early, that and the fact that my second year had many major happenings. Due to my being outside so much and talking with my guardian, I developed a very close relationship with trees and interestingly enough, storms. Later, when moving to a new area and away from my Grandparent's ranch, I developed an extremely close relationship with a large willow tree. Hiking with my family led to a relationship and many talks with Mount Lassen. Skiing fostered an extremely close relationship with Mount Shasta. These were all encouraged by my guardian, who was always with me when I would speak to the spirits.

I learned with my guardian how to gather an energy, a "something" that he sometimes called ki and to direct it. He often told me that it would help me when I was older because I could help others. I could also be in better control of myself "because sometimes your emotions cause things to happen around you, that when you are able to control yourself, your energy will not go toward... as much..." When I was sick, in addition to mother bringing me soup and making me drink water, she would put a hand on my head. At times, she would place her other hand elsewhere on my body as well. When she touched me, I could feel that aforementioned "something" flow through her and into me. My guardian and her guardian would often join her in doing this. Sometimes I would hear her pray, but that was rare, and the words changed each time. I have found this technique mentioned in the Bible, read many books about it, and even eventually found out about a Japanese equivalent which I have received a distance attunement to "re-awaken" and hope someday to receive in-person attunements to see what affect those will have on me in ability to work with this energy.

I do less ritual working now than I did when first consciously setting out and "officially" committing myself to the study and practice of magic, as a discipline in itself, at the age of nine. At that time, simple exercises and observations moved to more focused applications that looking back were quite ritualistic. I think that clearly demarcated steps helped my young mind understand better and have a firm grounding. Far fewer of my practices now are recognizably ritualistic, and are once again more "natural." They happen when they happen, and if using a physical focus, with what I have on hand. A protective circle will spring up when I feel I have need, though I can strengthen it by repeating familiar steps, as just one recent example.

Something that I take particular interest in is weather magic, which blends well with my work with dragons. Where I am living now is an agricultural area. The balance of rain, snow, and sun, and its effects on the livestock and crops has always fascinated me. I have been known to go out and dance to call the rains in a dry season, and have since I was very small. I must add that it isn't always successful, though I at least get a soft breeze. The breeze could easily be from just the way the atmosphere is working at the time, but the weather still interests me in how it shifts even minutely to a focused application. I have also been known to cry in frustration or sorrow, and then depending on how great it was, rain was known to follow. This was far more common in my childhood, though sometimes it seems that great joy when interacting with my mate also can help "feed" a storm.

I construct charm bags now and then and send them to people that need a "little something." I generally don't charge these with partners anymore. I find it easier to simply charge them myself than to set up a time to work with someone for such a simple task. The only times that I have charged a charm bag or token with any working partner was when both of us had an interest in the safety or well being of the recipient.

I also tend to write stories as part of my magical practices, as well as for stress relief, which is a type of magic in itself I've found. It is when going over the stories with the intention to share them with others that stress actually arises in the writing process for me. The stories that I write take the characters through the worlds as I see them and it is interesting to see how they either grow or dodge. This is also something that my guardian is supportive of, although he doesn't always get along completely from the thought forms that arise during the writing process. I've found the birth of some of these thought forms and their evolution into entities to be very interesting, as they can be called on for their qualities.

I sometimes wonder if I risk falling into a set gender role at times when matters of the hearth take the greatest slice of my attention, since so much hinges around life and growth. There is sometimes a temptation to fall solely into cooking and cleaning, where simple magics tie in so perfectly. Something always happens to make me pull back and eye my surroundings on all levels. This is when I look for traps of all sorts, as I have walked into traps before. I know too well what happens when complacency settles in and people around me being to take the things that I do out of love and concern for granted. I already know what it is to have no other reason for my existence than toward the dwelling. I already have been solely the "house and hearthkeeper," and have no wish to be "just that."

To become trapped, to become bound, to become merely a servant, that is a great fear of mine. As long as I am wary of whom it is around me, I know I will be fine. Even though I've not been taken advantage of magically except on a few occasions, I have learned to be wary due to instances in my mundane life. This is a lesson that I hope my daughter never has to learn the hard way, that I can teach her to avoid those traps. However, I know that she will make her own choices and probably similar mistakes. That is simply the way of life, and how we all learn.

Working Partners

I don't need a large group, much of what I do is solo work. On the other hand, my family and my loved ones are my group. If my daughter is feeling bullied, then depending on the situation we will do a working together after we have talked about what is going on and what she needs to do physically. If a family member is ill I will do a health working. My daughter or my mother may also participate with me, or do separate workings of their own if they choose to. My large extended family has also on occasion done group prayer for specific outcomes.

I have worked many years with cats and dogs as physical familiars. My very first familiar was a black long-hair cat who was born in 1993. When meditating, he would sit beside me. When performing candle spells, he would sit beside me, or on my desk. He would let me know when my father was coming to the door. When working outside, the large black dog that we had at the time would walk with me and stand guard. Both of these first familiars have since crossed over, but others have followed. One of those cats has come back several times, and the first cat once came back as a fish.

Among humans, I have mostly worked magic with other females, so I won't list them all. Growing up, and most of my life, that was who was most available to me. Father, understandably, was wary of me being alone with unrelated males. Due to this, and the resulting distrust of men that I learned, acts of magic I have only worked with perhaps three males in my life. The first of these was my former magical and religious training partner from junior high and high school. He was also my only male friend all those years ago. We still contact each other, and have been known to "send a flare" when we need to talk. The next was my then boyfriend in the last of my first year of college. This person is no longer in my life. The embodied male that I work with now is my mate, and each of these relationships has had very different sorts of workings.

I personally would like to think that the reason of the differences in workings is due to spiritual growth on my part. I have simply grown out of some of the practices, such as love spells, that I once participated in, or wish to think so. When I do work a love spell now, as an example, I work it from a different frame of mind. I also insist to do the work-spell with the person who has requested it. I stress to the requester that the purpose is not intended to attract a certain person, but to help the person bring the proper energies into their own life. An also stated side purpose would be to have the proper frame of mind to see the choices that are out there. Many years ago, I merely would have performed a spell to attract a named person on behalf of my client and left it at that.

With my first male working partner we covered a wide range. By the time of our senior year, we were meeting weekly. Our practices touched on stereotypical teenage love spells, to guided journeys, besom construction, and the afore-mentioned religious studies as well as much more. A spell that we performed that had great success was a booster protective spell for the creatures on my parents' property after the discovery of the murder of the previously mentioned dog. He had been found barely off the property.

My second introduced me briefly to how sexual energy can be used to heal, re-iterating my already known connection with dragons, as well as a few other lessons that I'm still not comfortable speaking of. My experience with the latter of these also lead to me being even more distrustful of males. This then paired with experiences in a romantic relationship that came after that relationship to result in a span of years before the last male working partner. It did not feel natural to me to not work magic with the person I was with during that span, who I left for trust reasons. I discovered that it was important to be able to have a mate that could be a working partner.

The only male that I work with now, not counting my guardian, is my mate. This is primarily from the frame of energetic transfers during particular situations. It tends to be equal exchange and not so much workings, as spontaneous encounters. There have been times where I have felt his essence visit me when I am not well. Often during those times that I am able to finally slip into a proper sleep. When I am aware of him not being well, I attempt the same for him as a return in love and gratitude. What I have observed our workings to focus on, in addition to energy exchange, are love and acceptance at very deep levels. This flows over into healing emotional and psychological wounds. In the course of our relationship, we have also found things in each other which remind us of ourselves, which has been an interesting process. This committed relationship, as well as being a magical one, has also taught me firsthand about the magical properties of personal psychology.

I have also done dream work with him, for the pleasure of his company as well as to pursue our intentions. Since we are currently separated by distance, it shows in our general waking feelings when something has caused us to not be able to meet on the dream plane. I am still not able to leave evidence of my presence in his room, but we are able to sense when our connection is weak. I also have developed a tendency to reach for him too often for mental protection when I feel vulnerable, sometimes to his dismay. He encourages me to be independent instead. This tendency to reach mentally and astrally for my mate first results in the slightly hurt feelings of my guardian as "that's what I'm here for."

I don't think this lack of opposite gender magical partners is due to segregation in the magical community. It's that I have never had reason to seek out any others after the core of my childhood working partners all moved into our own separate lives, in separate areas. That isn't to say that I don't work with them anymore. When I do, it is usually in the dream or astral worlds. If I feel a tug of need from them while in the physical/waking world, I will sit and lend my assistance. The fact that I tend to let people within my barriers to different levels while working with them probably also adds to my "periodic and situational hermit-like tendencies."

I also don't include in this essay the people that I have worked with regarding psychic research and practice. To me, though they certainly cross over at many points, magic and psychic powers fork off from each other at certain points, which though I'd love to try and graph just for the visual reference of my beliefs, it escapes me every time I try to.

Teresa Garcia

Community

As mentioned earlier, I have learned to be careful who I speak with. Some of the reasons I would never have thought possible when I was a pre-teen. I expected a bit of prejudice, for reasons of being different from my community of origin, and I was right. I have expected people to try to convert me from one path to another, and the attempts have been many. Not everyone has attempted to sway me, but enough for me to be wary. I don't think that I encounter any problems from merely being female regarding spiritual and magical prejudice. If so, it has been so slight or so long ago that it has been put out of mind.

Something that I should have expected, and did not, was that people of one spiritual/magical path in particular would ask me to band with them to "correct" mistakes of everyone's practices. I see no reason to be correcting anyone's practices unless their magical practices involved taking the life of someone. So I am always bothered if someone comes to me asking me to change something about another person's practices. Unless it brings harm such as sacrificing someone's firstborn, it's not my business and I'm more than happy not to get pulled into it.

Prejudice, when encountered against myself, I have found more in day to day life than in any magical involvements. Much of the time, being a small woman, I can see how I am easily overlooked and underestimated. Perhaps my lack of experience in this area comes from the fact that when I do network, it is in very small, close communities, and usually on the Internet. Or it could come from having grown in a very small and isolated community. I'm of mixed races and heritages, but I look white unless I'm wearing something that people associate more with a race or heritage, or a person looks for particular genetic traits. As "white" or "Caucasian" is dominant in this area, that could be a factor and thus I "blend in."

I am very much a loner regarding some of my practices, and there are certain aspects that only my mate will be allowed to know. Certain parts that even if he wished to know, I have no way to explain to him at this time. Although I love words, until he reaches a point where he will grasp the ideas I work with on his own, I can't share those with even him. I simply lack the ability to convey most of what I think to anyone through any medium other than writing or artwork. I am content with this, as it is the way of the world, or at the very least my world.

Words Spoken Beneath the Willow

I also don't see why, if someone were to push to be included in my practices, I should accept them in unless I found them to be someone that I can work well with. This is in part a trust issue. I don't do anything ground shaking, so it hasn't been a problem. I've not had people come pounding on my door, and those that have asked me that I haven't felt like I could work with I've been able to turn away or get away from. Perhaps I've not always been able to discourage those few easily, but I did manage. Some people that I've networked with, I've fallen away from because of communication problems and differences in intent.

Where I currently live, which is where I grew up, magic and/or psychic gifts wasn't usually something talked about openly. When it was, it was usually discussed in religious terms. If you worked in a group, it was a very small group to escape ridicule or to protect your beliefs if they were not the norm. With this in mind, though I can now network with more people, I really don't think I could work well with a larger group. I simply have too much personal baggage and probably too many trust issues, and a few issues regarding a particular religion that I am currently working on healing. It still isn't an area where you can talk openly, say, at the Frosty on the corner, but it is slowly evolving. I am aware of a church there that now accepts that everyone is given gifts.

Sometimes, I do wish for a larger community, magically speaking. It would be nice to talk to others more often about these subjects, and be accepted. But in keeping things small, it is easier for me. It prevents me from making hugely glaring mistakes that get me involved with the wrong sort of person. But I know that there are others out there, I see them from time to time when I go to the bigger towns or cities.

I see younger ones on the Internet, just starting out, caught up in the glamour before they realize that magic isn't something flashy that solves all problems in an instant. I sometimes am reminded of a card I have on my working altar. It is of a young Native American woman, a Storm Maiden, playing in the clouds with lightning as it rains. I often wonder how long it will be before they learn that to control that lightning takes work, that to turn it to a use takes effort. I know that if I speak and say it, that I will be pooh-poohed as some old woman who is afraid or can't.

I still am very much a Storm Maiden, though if anyone wants to be technical, I'm a Storm Mother too, and I've zapped myself a fair number of times. That's my element, and here we could easily cross into my religious life, but that would be a subject for another essay. I remember what it was like when younger, and that is another part of why I think I would be considered to be somewhere on the fringe of the so-called magical community. Things have changed since I first left my home and eventually found my way into the "community," only to withdraw to the edge where it's fairly quiet. But I am here, in the shadows, behind the screen, in the trees or the crystalline caverns, and the raging storms. I am a woman, a magic worker, a mother, a daughter, a partner, and a sister. When I do come out of hiding enough to be seen and to be heard, it is because I think I might have something to add, and that is a rare thing.

I know I am not the only one, and it is ok. We don't all have to be just like each other, or part of some "accredited" brother/sisterhood. Everyone is different, and everyone has a different path because of this. Of course, this is all my experience, and you may be one of those that doesn't believe in dragons, or soul embraces across vast miles at night, or trying to bring rain to end a bad drought, or telepathy or anything similar. But I hope we can both agree that life is a pretty magical thing. We all have some similarity somewhere.

Biography

Teresa Garcia is a twenty nine year old Storm Priestess and Witch who grew up in the mountains of Northern California, in a rural community. She is the mother of two children and now lives happily in another rural community. From early childhood she has lived closely with Gods, Dragons, and Spirits. She swore her life to the path of a storm priestess since the late 90's, and sometime after the birth of her second child sought to attain legal clergy status at the nudging of her Deities. Teresa performs general clergy services to those who request her help, mostly weddings/handfastings and funerals. She has written one book of spiritual poetry, and two spiritual/adventure novels for her ongoing Dragon Shaman series. Her most recent book, *The Smoky Mirror*, is expected to be released in September of 2009.

COVE-WITCHES AND CURANDERAS: TRADITIONAL HEALERS AND MAGIC-WOMEN IN MODERN APPALACHIA
BYRON BALLARD

I come from a family of Appalachian witches on my mother's side. My grandmother self-identified and was identified by friends and fellow choir members as a witch. She had precognitive dreams and seemed to know things before they happened. She had a special warning dream that she never told anyone the specifics of and when she called you to say she'd had The Dream, you paid attention because her dreams were never wrong. This strain of witchcraft runs back several generations in our family oral history--but no one lists witchcraft on Census forms, so ancestrydotcom is no help in my quest to find out how far back these women were considered witches. It seems to fall along the English branch of the family, the Irish branch given only to singing, drink and bad temper.

I was told that I would get a "gift" when I grew up, a family gift, like my grandmother's dreams or my great-grandmother's healing power. My mother always thought the gift had skipped her and I could never tell if she was wistful or relieved about that. When I was young, though, I remember my mother being fascinated by ghosts and we would go ghost-hunting sometimes on the weekends, bundling up in the old pink Buick to drive to some place my mother had heard was haunted. Our home place had the ghost of the old man who built it--Mr. Haney--who would clear his throat outside in the yard, early in the morning and my mother always heard him. My grandmother moved to a tall house in the city and it was haunted and is haunted still by a ghost named Mrs. Brown, a ghost my sister-in-law has seen on several occasions and isn't a "she" at all.

Nowadays, we would say that my mother's gift was the ability to recognize discarnate spirits but we didn't have fancy words for what we were and what we did. Some folks had the healing, some folks had the seeing, some could stop a flow of blood by reading a verse from the Bible. My mama liked spooks. It didn't seem weird or particularly unnatural--there were plenty of neighbors who also had abilities like that--we called them granny-women and cove doctors, sometimes.

But mostly we called them Mamaw or Mz. Swanger or Old Lady Boyd. They knew a baby had to have a silver dime on a string around her neck to make it easy for teeth to cut through. They knew if you didn't give an infant catnip tea then hives would break out on the inside and kill her. They knew about spring tonics and poultices, about what greens you could eat. I learned the burn spell from them, though they didn't call it a spell. It was just the words you said if somebody had a bad burn, and then the burn got better.

I learned healing techniques from these women, when and how to plant a garden, how to divine the weather and to read an ordinary deck of playing cards to see the future. It wasn't fancy. It didn't require a special outfit or special ritual tools. It is a down-home witchcraft that is simple and effective. Something that comes naturally and uses materials at hand. It is based on generations of living close to the land and being poor and making do.

In my part of the world, it is also a woman's work. The cove women who practice it are respected, honored and a little feared. Rarely have men interfered in this work or participated in it.

We know from anthropological studies that witchcraft is cross-cultural and is the practice of peasant medicine and psychology. My family never saw witchcraft as their religion. They were Methodists--my great-grandfather was one of the founders of a Methodist church and my grandmother's second husband was a lay minister. As a Wiccan priestess, I am both a lower-case and an upper case witch/Witch--I got a double dose of witching, an extra helping, as it were. I call what I learned and what I do hillfolk hoodoo, with a nod towards those other hoodoos that are practiced around America, as well as the hoodoos that came from the in-migration of different people into these mountains. (In "Hoodoo origin and Thoughts on Etymology & Dictionary Makers" Bill Cassleman quotes from Daniel Cassidy, founder of An Léann Éireannach, who traces the word "hoodoo" to Irish; "uath dubh", "dark shape".) Kitchen witchery, some call it. But "hoodoo" suits me--I think of it as a special set of abilities and talents reserved for folks like me. Hillfolks.

We sit at a great crossroads here in the southern Appalachian mountains. The Scots-Irish came into this place centuries ago and swapped lore and culture with the Cherokee and the Creek. African slaves brought their own brand of healing and psychology to the land and that added to the base of herb lore and other odd knowledge. For decades now, there have been Mexican migrant workers in the southern mountains--they came in to pick the fall apple crops. But now they have come to reside in the mountains and they bring their own kind of witchery.

What is hillfolk hoodoo--the kind that's practiced in the southern highlands of Appalachia? And how is like or unlike the traditional healing practiced by the newest immigrants to this region, the Latino folks? It's medicine and midwifery, it's omen-reading and weather working. Sometimes it requires the witch to have a listening ear and an open heart: she may be asked to give advice or to keep a secret. It's working in both the physical realm and in the psychological one, using keen observation, common sense, experience and folkways to affect change.

Because of women in those two coves--and in Benson Holler on the other side of the woods from where my cousin Dena lived--I practice a kind of witchcraft that is natural and easy. When I am called on to help someone with a health issue or a relationship issue, I can brew up a cup of tea and talk it through. When I am called because someone feels their house is haunted, I load up a little basket of salt and grits and vervain and corn liquor and I head out the door to do some Appalachian feng shui. I have become the village witch for much of my community and when I say "my community" I am not only talking about the Pagans and Wiccans who are my co-religionists, I am also talking about the regular folks in my neighborhood who feel like they need a change of luck or who want to know what kind of tincture they should take for hives. I have become an urban cove doctor, though I don't say wise-woman. Somehow that sounds fancier than what I do and less honest.

I have done some work for local Mexican and South American migrants, using a sympathetic Catholic priest as translator. These people long for the comfort and familiarity of curanderismo and though I don't speak their language, they know what I'm doing. At a favorite local restaurant, the waiter calls me "brujita" with some affection and a little respect. I correspond with a woman in San Antonio to learn more about trabajos and I look forward to the day when we have a real botanica here. Have you tried the Amazing Rue Candle? The name is certainly apt.

Coming up through the re-birthing of religious Paganism in the 1970s, we often downsized these humble arts in an attempt to seem more like the ceremonial magicians we read about, as we aspired to have a lineage. Those were the days when wearing a big flashy pentacle and taking a magical name were standard and we stood in perfectly-cast circles, with salt and chalices, wearing robes and crowns.

Maybe we all return to our roots in the end, searching for the sustenance in our magic work that gives the work power and meaning within the context of our communities. I do still stand in circle sometimes, wearing my crown and best robes. But more often than not, my magical work--and the magical work of most of the women I know who think of themselves as witches--involves a sincere offering to the spirits of the land and our Ancestors, some homegrown herbs dried on the porch and a perfectly-brewed cup of tea. My lineage is in my blood and my bones, and in the sparse soil of these old hills.

Biography

H. Byron Ballard holds a MFA from Trinity University (theatre) and a BA from UNC-Asheville (drama). She is a ritualist, teacher, speaker and writer. Byron has been a practicing witch since the early 1970s and a Wiccan priestess since 1975. She serves on the Triskele of the Mother Grove Temple project, a non-profit multifaith organization whose goal is to raise a Goddess Temple. Byron does interfaith work with the United Religions Initiative and the Mountain Area Interfaith Forum, as well as creating public rituals for each of the Wiccan holydays.

Her published writing has appeared in WNC Woman Magazine, the Mountain Xpress, Carolina Home & Garden Magazine, Verve Magazine, in PanGaia and the Black Mountain Review. Two of her essays are featured in "Birthed from Scorched Hearts" ("The Daughters of Boudicca") from Fulcrum Press and "Christmas Presence" ("A Season of Light: How We Celebrated a Hillbilly Yule") by a local press. She has essays and articles on Wicca and other earth-focused spiritualities at the Witches Voice website, Global Goddess Oracle ezine, and Matrifocus.

She blogs for Gannett as "the Village Witch" (www.citizen-times.com/village witch) and authored a pamphlet for Pagan converts called "Back to the Garden: a Handbook for New Pagans" that has been widely distributed.

Byron is currently at work on "Earth Works: Eight Ceremonies for the Coming Changes" She lives in Asheville, NC with her husband Joe and daughter Kate.

WHAT I HOLD IN MY HAND
KRIS LEET

I have begun the seventh decade of my current life. Just typing this fact fills me with awe, with amazement. I am becoming old! I have waited all my life to be old, to have salt and pepper hair, to be free of the restraints of living a sexually defined role, to have the long view that brings some semblance of understanding, to be fierce and perhaps, eventually, wise. Such were the grandmothers and great-grandmothers of my childhood, the women who kept the hearth fires, remembered the stories, and listened when the mothers were too busy with demands of the husbands and the world.

I am a witch. Not a pagan, not a practitioner of natural religion, not a Wiccan. A witch. I am interested in power; the power to connect to what I deem sacred, the power to embody the divine, the power to enact my will, the power to willingly and on purpose participate in and shape the energy and form around me.

I am also a mother, a grandmother, a daughter, sister, therapist, researcher, artist, anthropologist, bisexual, educated, left-of-center, white woman. I am an initiated priestess and elder in a number of magickal traditions.

I tell you these things because my thinking has been shaped by what and who I am, by what has been done to me and what I have done. My experiences are what I know, and how I know it. The older I get the more I trust my experience as valid knowledge. What I am going to say now is my experience, what I have come to know filtered through who I am.

I came to magick in isolation and silence. Not the isolation of the little girl who knew telling anyone she could swing on a certain branch from a certain tree before entering the apple orchard and make everything different was a bad idea, but the isolation of one who thinks that magick as a practiced art is no longer alive in the world, that one was born too late. Not the silence of keeping oath-bound secrets but the silence of whispered voices not yet clear enough to decipher. I read the old books when I could find them, haunted the fringes where folk traditions still held sway, and continued to cautiously enter changed places and look for clues. I found them. I cobbled them together, tested their strength, their veracity and power, and made up a working explanation for how things fit together, how the magickal world made sense to me and how I could use that knowledge to effect my will.

Magick and weaving have pervaded my life, as separate daily pursuits, as metaphors for each other, and as strands of the same fabric, each embellishing the other. Weaving is the process of taking separate, disparate elements and intertwining them in ways that make them a singular, unified whole connected by an underlying structure that carries the desired combination of pattern, color and texture. Magick, too, is a making; the identification of individual strands of energy, the separation of those strands from the background of the energic tapestry of the universe, and the construction of a new structure that manifests and supports the will and vision of the magician.

Weavers expect to create something from nothing, to start with a handful of floppy strings barely able to bear their own weight and end up with a strong, flexible fabric able to withstand centuries of use. Every weaver has their own, recognizable "hand". No two weavers, no matter how skilled, can create the same cloth. Each fabric will have a different feel; a unique blend of materials, technique, and experience.

One part of my magickal life is the magick I made up, the magick that found me. It was made the way one weaves. It was created in the place it inhabited, shaped by the geometry of the land and the hand that held it. It was the product of an experiential interaction, a dialogue between the sacred and the person encountering the sacred. That encounter was elaborated, described, moved from internal to external space, embodied in rituals, invocations, spells; a magickal system, if you will, based upon personal experience, personal revelation. It is my favorite garment, always worn next to my skin regardless of what else I wear.

Weavers also expect to do a certain amount of repair work: fix a broken thread, strengthen a worn patch, re-weave the place the puppy chewed when no one was looking. Most weavers are the recipients of a host of in-need-of-repair items lovingly brought by friends, or discarded, unwanted items left on the doorstep by unseen strangers. They do their best to re-make the item, returning them to their original condition: fully functional, structure and embellishment intact.

In a magickal sense I am a Keeper. As a Keeper it is my task to preserve, maintain, and repair, if necessary, that which is put in my care. In most cases that simply means enacting the rituals I have been given, letting them deepen and expand my understanding, ensuring that they be not lost or forgotten, and being vigilant about where one set of understandings stops and another begins. I assume, rightly I hope, that all magickal practitioners do this for the traditions to which they are initiated. May it be so!

Traditions are living things, a fact that as magickally aware people we should know and honor. They must be nourished, petted, bathed, played with, shared, or they become twisted and petulant, bitter, psychotic, or languish and die. In my experience traditions on the verge of being maltreated or forgotten desperately seek someone to keep them, to nurture, preserve, and maintain them until they can be shared again. In several cases I have been the one such traditions dropped in upon while waiting for a more permanent home.

In the first case it was a total surprise, unexpected and alarming. One moment I was a regular person sitting in an outer court class and the next I was responsible for the maintenance and repair of a very noisy and demanding tradition, not the one, I might add, that was being presented. It was an accident, borne of inexperience on my part and hubris on the part of another. It changed my life forever, taught me more than I intended to know, and set a pattern for my magickal life.

The second case was planned. I knew I was accepting responsibility for an incomplete magickal system that no longer knew where it had come from. The priest who had initiated my initiator was probably dead. My initiator had months to live. Much of the written materials had been lost and what was remembered was being lost to disease and the effects of treatment. What remained was so unique, so unlike anything I had ever seen, and so poignant and pure that I was willing to preserve it and try to remember the rest.

What does it mean to fix or repair a magickal tradition? For me it means attempting to identify the energy signature of that tradition, clear away all the debris that has accumulated or attached itself to that signature, and then ensure that the energy is encapsulated in a vessel of ritual, spell, recipe and technique that support, nurtures, and enacts the unique energy of the tradition. Once that is done the forms must be obeyed and enacted frequently to feed and maintain the tradition, and fuel the work to be done. The tradition is then ready to be properly shared again.

In the first case, the tradition that just dropped from the sky, so to speak, there was a lot of material available, including former practitioners of the tradition, at least one complete Book of Shadows, and a set of diaries. There were also the voices of various deities with their own critique and set of suggestions for "setting it aright". I spent a year annotating the rituals, documenting where the various pieces had come from and how they had been changed. I read more ceremonial and far-flung early magickal books than one can imagine, talked to people who had practiced or knew people who had practiced the tradition, read books about the tradition (it was, remains, infamous). I found a skillful and willing priest to help and we did all of the original rituals as written, then the first and second set of re-writes done by the founders, identifying what threads moved through both. Always the questions concerned what was authentic and what was intended.

After years of work we did our own rewrite. Our focus was to create rituals we could ethically perform while keeping the energy of the tradition pure and true to itself. Simultaneously we corrected, at the instruction of the deities involved, some of the less than fortunate choices made by early practitioners that trapped and putrefied the energy raised in ritual. We invited former members and friends of the original circle to do ritual with us and offer an opinion about whether or not we had retained the traditional energy while cleaning up the problems.

One of our advantages was that we had not been on the original circle, which was created when the founders were in their twenties. All of the emotional baggage of being twenty-something, sexually involved, and in the middle of the early drug culture as well as powerfully linked magically blinded the remaining members to both the miscalculations they had made and the incredible beauty and elegance of what they had created. In the end we were able to return their creation to them clean of all of that, brilliant once more. The tradition has since flourished.

In the second case, the tradition that was incomplete, the process requires that the remaining rituals and spells be enacted, that the ritual gestures be done and the words be spoken frequently enough that one can hold the energy in ones hand long enough to feel its pulse. Research, too, is needed. Research about the where the founding mythology, all unverifiable, says the tradition comes from, who the people where who used the tradition, what language the spells are in, and if there is anything out there that looks like it. The book, such as it is, must be shared with other elders so that their knowledge and contacts can be consulted. Every time an elder tells me that they have never seen the like before convinces me that we magicians need this knowledge; every time an elder points me toward a person or source of related material I rejoice in the connections made and the clues found. My desire is to foster the tradition until it is itself again, whatever that might be rather than to shape it into what is familiar or comfortable.

This is a work in progress, just barely begun, begun in fits and starts. I was initiated and my initiator died within months. She was able to witness the initiation of a priest who agreed to take on the work of reconstruction before her death. We know, from her mouth and our own experience, that I was able to pass the energy given to her by her initiator to my initiate. So we start with little more than the energy of that line that I can hold in my hand. In addition, I have a few recipes, a number of spells, some of which are complete free-standing rituals, and an initiation ritual, and Samhain ritual. There are a few notes which may or may not be connected to the tradition. We have deity names that no one recognizes, we have circle castings unlike any I have ever seen. We have a tradition with one initiation only, and some allusions to elder recognition when the established elders perceive that the magick has pervaded your life and informed your knowing.

The foundation myth suggests that the tradition originated in the Appalachian Mountains, that the man who initiated my initiator, an outlander, was "recognized" for what he was by a family or group of families when he lived there and brought into the group. I have no verification of this and make no claim about the truth of this story other than I respect without reservation my initiator and have no reason to doubt that she believed this to be the truth.

Whether this story is true or not I do not know. What I do know is that there is power and beauty in the rituals, power and energy in the initiation, and lively dialogue between the deities and their people. In the end that is all we ever have. Our experience, my experience, and the knowledge it brings. Trust yourself to weave what you desire, to mend what you value, to fix what matters. It is enough that it is what you know to be authentic, it is enough that it is your experience.

Magick and weaving. They are inseparable in my life. When I weave the magick flows. When I do magick the strands appear in my hands and intertwine about each other as I desire and intend.

Biography

Kris is a master weaver, artist, elder, author, and researcher. Her current passions include women's magick, weaving in the Dark

Ages, Neolithic religion, and spending time with her family and friends.

SPEAKING AS A WOMAN

Women working magic face the same issues that women face everywhere. Magical women can abuse others, and can be abused. Women may find themselves alone in groups of men working a particular kind of magic. They may struggle to redefine magical practice after a trauma or injury.

The stories in this section are personal tales from magical lives. Some of them are inspiring, some thought provoking, some are raw and powerful. All come from the writer's individual experiences of magic. Grace Victoria Swann, Erynn Rowan Laurie, Jaymi Elford, Mordant Carnival, and myself all discuss the impact being gendered a woman has had on our magical lives. Each voice here uncovers an issue that affects many other women on the magical paths. Each looks forward to the future, outlining the next step we foresee, and expressing our hopes for ourselves, and by extension our hopes for the lives of other women, and people of all genders, on the magical paths.

THE ACCIDENTAL MAGICIAN
GRACE VICTORIA SWANN

"You have done the right thing coming here," she said, touching my hand slightly and staring me squarely in the face as if to give me a burst of confidence with a single look.

She said I was "lucky". But to be honest, I was just numb.

She handed me a Diet Coke. "Everything is going to be okay. He won't hurt you anymore."

She stood up, and turned, shutting the door behind her. Leaving me alone.

The sound of my breathing and beat of my heart drowned out the ringing of telephones and the hum of a ceiling fan, moving the stagnant institutional air.

The Power Of Kali

My hands shook as I wrote details of activities that took place just hours before on a piece of paper. I'd never had trouble writing before, but knowing that whatever I wrote was going to be reviewed by a plethora of law enforcement officials made me lock up.

I wasn't just writing my story. It was "my statement ". It was evidence, the same as the photographs that had been taken of the unwelcome bruises on my body -- proof of restraint, of hands squeezing my neck, marks of impact on my legs and arms, and of forceful slaps across my face – reddened, pocked, skin sensitive to the touch. The whiplash didn't photograph, but was documented in the hospital records. And the house was destroyed – a broken table, wine on the ceiling, plumbing ripped out of one of the bathroom walls, holes from him -- punching walls and thrusting a chair at me in a moment of anger.

Tears streamed down my cheeks as I retraced what I could remember in detail. The image of the man that had four months earlier promised to "love, honor and cherish" me was firmly replaced with a new persona. The latest was a monster – shaking me, yelling at the top of his lungs -- his lips only inches from my face, the tingle of my cheek after a hard slap and the words "You stupid, stupid, woman!!!" trilling off his lips in repetition.

This wasn't the way life was supposed to work out. He was supposed to be my partner in love, in life and in magick.

His strange behavior began much earlier in our relationship, but I didn't see the signs consistently to the point where I could act with confidence. Before this turn for the worse, he was in one breath frustrating and fascinating. His words made me feel like heaven and hell. One minute he was hugging me – the next punching a hole in the wall and calling me names. I wrote off his initial threats of physical harm, but when the moment came that he finally turned I called on support.

It was like living on a roller coaster. I couldn't stay on; I couldn't get off.

My unexpected pregnancy pushed him over the edge. I learned that some men snap quickly after marriage, learning of pregnancy or even becoming a parent. Statistically these are triggers for some men, causing them to go off a deep end.

The police helped get the ball rolling with his arrest and short-term incarceration. A battered women's non-profit group helped me off the crazy ride and started helping me to make sense of life again.

Yes, I was lucky, but I also felt so lost. My voice had been silenced for so long even I could not hear it.

I'd listened to the same message from the pulpit week after week during my childhood and formative years. The messages were filled with poison of my "imperfection". I was "unclean" I was woman – never to be made whole while I was alive. I was inherently flawed and to strive for perfection was fruitless, even blasphemous. Men and women were made to make each other "complete".

Despite abandoning my conservative Christian roots long ago, there was still a piece of me that adhered to the concept of "submitting" to a man. The culture I lived in, the south, only cemented this weakened part of me. Talking about myself – my thoughts, ideas, and accomplishments -- was viewed as prideful. I was supposed to "be nice".

Even at business meetings with a Bachelors degree under my belt and awards on my walls, new colleagues would start up conversations asking about my "other half" instead of about my skills, talents and abilities.

In that culture I often wished I had a penis – not just for those business meetings, but for the opportunity to get a better price on haircuts and dry cleaning.

But it wasn't just the cultural encoding that built me up and broke me down, the tumultuous two-year ride of romance ripped apart my insides. I'd never had a love before that was concerned with spiritual matters. He'd introduced me to the occult arts – brought me into a coven, introduced me to (what I thought at the time was) Ceremonial Magick. In return, I was supposed to be his silent, non-questioning partner – the woman that made the cocktails, assured the buffet table was set and adorned for feast, and who also worked two jobs to pay the bills because he couldn't find work or keep a job for more than about a month without being canned. I kept his secrets and played the martyr.

As an occultist, he sold himself as more experienced than me – more knowledgeable than me and he backed his stance with words and phrases that I, honestly, never checked out. I took him at his word. Fool that I was. If I had a theory, a thought, an idea, it was "incorrect" and I was quickly informed – with often-contradictory terms, weakening me through confusion. Feeling I'd be lost without him, I gave him cart blanche to my finances – added his name to the house and gave him credit cards. I trusted him to be true, to be good, to honor his promises – despite the contrary behavior.

And that day, at the police station, I began questioning everything.

The Gifts of Saraswati

Investigation revealed things to me in layers, further increasing my feelings of personal failure and shame. Knowledge gave me sporadic power, lessening my feelings of helplessness.

In reality, my husband *(thinking of him in those terms now makes my skin crawl)* had serious mental disturbances. As a magician his true repertoire only consisted of parroting the Book of the Law. The rituals he claimed that he wrote were really phrases ripped straight out of the Gnostic Mass, put in a different setting. The armchair magician waxing philosophic put him squarely in the center of attention, which made women either fawn over him or become repulsed by his narcissism.

The first night he was in jail, after the locksmith arrived to change the locks on all the doors, I finally had momentary peace and the beginnings of a feeling of waking up from a bad dream.

Drugs kept me functioning at my job and allowed me periods of sleep. A claw hammer and kitchen knife became my new bedtime partners, until I woke up one morning bleeding, having cut my hand on the blade during my sleep.

Taking a stance with regards to my new life situation, the coven folk with whom I'd previously worked magick told me that my soon to be ex was no longer welcome. I was instructed to continue transcribing the Book of Shadow's I'd been given; to work ritual outside as often as possible and to do whatever it took to protect myself. *(The judge signed restraining order was minimally effective until it was broken a fourth time.)*

A couple friends living at a nearby river allowed me use of their yards and kept a watchful eye on me while I wrote, and wrote, and wrote – transcribing words in an aspiration to eventually become a second degree Alexandrian Witch. First degree had been absolute hell. I wanted into the next domain as quickly as I could get there, while still remaining onto sanity.

Another friend became my roommate and constant companion. A filmmaker with great imagination, he was open to my sword wielding and fire burning without wrinkling a brow.

I exercised like a fiend, and was given some books to grow my occult library, which allowed me access to different materials and varying perspectives. My finances destroyed and on the verge of bankruptcy, I dared not make such purchases for myself.

I began to feel like a mutation of Humpty Dumpty merging with a Jedi Knight in training.

I'd often sing Sheryl Crowe's song "It Don't Hurt" at the top of my lungs during this time, patching holes and painting walls with $5 a gallon Oops! paint... putting my literal and figurative house in order.

It don't hurt like it did
I can sing my song again

I scraped the paper off the wall
I put down carpet in the hall
I left no trace of you at all
And I can sing my song again

The months of healing that followed revealed something I'd neglected to notice before. In my state of tumult, I'd often write in my journal. Nothing unusual, per se, I'd kept a journal since the fifth grade – the results of an English assignment turned into a habit.

But the content was different from year's past – from the meanderings of other times of life, love and youth. My journal had become my only true safe space when I had been in relationship. And in hindsight, trying to make sense of the choices I'd made, I flipped through pages. Revealed were patterns of divination, details of trips away when I'd work magick alone in my hotel room, spells I'd written, dreams I'd had and experiments I'd conducted – from the mountains of Tennessee – to the beaches of Florida. I'd not shared these experiences, details or reflections with my supposed partner in magick – or with anyone else.

Why the silence? I was fearful of being judged. Other people knew more than me. I was woman – incomplete and flawed. Of course, the magick I worked had to be too…right?

Perhaps not.

Like a baby crawls before it can walk, I merely was learning to flap my wings before I could fly. And akin to a baby bird, I'd simply fallen to the ground and been tormented by a neighborhood tomcat.

But something was effective with regards to the magick I'd worked alone. In order for the magick to fulfill the full will of intent, however, I had to leave the southeast. After months of legal postponements, my ex pled guilty to breaking the protective orders. He'd linked up with another woman, who I believe, was encouraging him to do whatever he could for things to be over. He was never brought up on charges for the assault or attempted strangulation. An administrative error had taken place and the paperwork sat on someone's desk for months, before finding its way back into the file folder after a new assistant District Attorney took office. I was told that for the sake of my own mental health it was best for me to move on. "Let it go for now." In some ways it was good that he hadn't been charged. When he did this to another woman, the dangling case would still be there – like a rope for him to hang himself.

Lakshmi's Fruits

I moved in October to the Midwest. Samhain was powerful; I'd communed that evening with the spirit of Moina Mathers – full of encouragement: "you are embarking on a period of great discovery…what unfolds will greatly benefit those who are ready to listen."

The Accidental Magician

My journal entry December 30, 2007 reads "with ritual, love and rest, I am healing...things that once didn't make sense at all now do. It's like pieces of a puzzle are beginning to snap together."

In the pieces snapping, lifetime dreams have started to come to fruition — the opportunity to be an author, to continue my education, and a trusted friend who's walked with me through some difficult times, has turned into my lover and partner. Although he's got more than 35 years documented occult experience and has spawned more than half a dozen still operating magickal groups he considers me a peer. We debate technique, structure, and spend many weekend hours with our heads buried in words. Apparently, I'd learned some things on my own, that I didn't realize had value initially - mostly through a love of reading and visiting different cultures around the globe.

After a period of fasting, meditation and having been given a new magickal name and specific call to service, I was elevated to third degree status as an Alexandrian witch during new moon in June of 2008. As is typical when I'm in a magickal setting, the ritual was simultaneously humbling and empowering. For me, this type of magick leaves me feeling empowered with courage - to move forward and take action. Messages are given, gifts of discernment.

I spend equal amounts of time practicing alone and with others, sometimes my partner/lover and other times in larger group settings to expose myself to different thoughts, beliefs and traditions. When solo, I utilize an organic mutation of Eastern and Western Magickal systems. A form of energetic magick akin to some of Franz Bardon's practices aids in the creation of powerful intent and accompanying verbiage - as well as provides me with tools for healing others, while staying grounded. British Traditional Wicca methodologies aid in establishing sacred space, complete with quarters, elements and seasonal cycles. Cross quarters, drawing various geometric structures with my body parts, sigils and talismans are periodic features of higher ritual magick workings I may perform - working with an assortment of deities or angels.

Holding things together is automatic writing. Sometimes I write until I pass out and wake up hours later in a puddle of my own drool.

I stink at verbal memorization; so much of what I do is put to song - whether in setting sacred space and calling quarters, or invoking through chant.

After beginning to work magick more intensely, my menstrual cycle morphed - ovulation during new moon, menstruation during full moon – allowing a full embodiment of women's mysteries through internal and external form. I saw this as positive – connecting me even more with a larger life force, allowing me to ride a wave.

At one time I tried to control the elements, now I just set intent and allow nature to take course, knowing that the destination will be reached.

For now, I still choke on most of Crowley's words as if they are a vile poison – forced down my throat in a previous incarnation of myself. I'm mustering up courage to visit the local OTO, realizing that when I can actually be in the same room with the words used in the Gnostic Mass again, it will indicate an additional level of healing. But for now, I'm not there. My ex used to say "Do what thou wilt" just before he screwed someone over. My knee-jerk internal response became "and step over the dead bodies..."

I may be off the roller coaster, but I'm still finding my way to a different part of the amusement park. I still hear echoes of the past, but keep walking with my eyes forward.

For a more than a year now, I've been gaining great strength working with various Hindu deities. While I realize that some may have opinion about mixing systems to this extreme, for me it makes perfect sense for now – destruction (Kali) leads to knowledge (Saraswati) and results in (Lakshmi) material and spiritual prosperity.

The natural alchemy of women is often silenced in our Western culture. Looking back, I am not proud of how I handed myself over. Fortunately, magick has given me the tools, resources and perspectives to create a new life.

We always have the power to redefine ourselves, but sometimes life's lessons take us to the foundation of our being, before we are given what we need to begin building anew.

Excerpts from an automatic writing message received full moon, December 2008:
Respect yourself and honor your boundaries; others will follow.
Let your anger and vengeance bring you laughter, not pain.
It will spring you further than ever imagined.
The paradox of trusting no one and everyone at the same time is perhaps the greatest lesson in self-preservation and growth.
Release it all and hold nothing back.
Be recklessly bold and follow through.
And visit me often for nourishment and strength.

Biography

Grace Victoria Swann is a witch, student and freelance writer/editor living in the Minneapolis, MN area with her partner, Frater Barrabbas. From Cherokee and German/Lutheran ancestry, Grace began formal studies in Witchcraft and High Magick in 2005. She recently attained 3rd degree in British Traditional Wicca (Alexandrian) and is active in the Order of the Gnostic Star, or Egregora Sancta Stella Gnostica (E.S.S.G.). Grace writes a quarterly pagan travel column for The Crooked Path Journal.

HIS MOTHER'S WHOLE BODY HEALS: GENDER AND RITUAL IN THE EKKLESÍA ANTÍNOOU
ERYNN ROWAN LAURIE, MYSTES, LUP. SEC.

In its inception the cult of Antinous, the deified lover of the Roman emperor Hadrian, is intentionally and intensely queer. Early Christian theologians and apologists attacked the religion in part because of the homoerotic nature of Hadrian and Antinous's relationship.[6] Even Julian, famously apostate, who embraced a return to Paganism after rejecting the Christianity in which he was raised, attacked the deification and worship of Antinous.[7]

Antinous was the last of the classical deities. His death in the Nile at the age of nineteen during late 130 CE at the festival of Osiris brought him traditional Egyptian deification and identification with the dead and risen god. This tradition was embraced and spread by Hadrian in his grief at his young lover's drowning. Temples were founded and an entire city, Antinoöpolis, was founded at Besa where the death occurred.[8] The worship of Antinous continued for at least two centuries after Hadrian's own death.

In much of the modern cult of Antinous, he is postulated specifically as a god of male homosexuality. One group presents him as a deity of gay triumphalism, declaring him the singular, monotheistic deity for gay men with no other worshippers or deities encouraged.[9] Such a position can be seen as taking coming out theology -- the idea that "it's okay to be gay" -- to its rather literalist and fundamentalist conclusion. This theological position led to a schism and the formation of the Ekklesía Antínoou: a more open and welcoming organization that encourages membership and

---

[6] See examples in Royston Lambert, *Beloved and God: The Story of Hadrian and Antinous* (New York: Viking, 1984), pp. 193-194.
[7] Lambert, pp. 192-193.
[8] Lambert, pp. 198-208.
[9] http://www.antinopolis.org/

activity by people of all sexualities and identities.[10] This history is important in contextualizing issues of gender and sexualities in modern Antinoan practice.

Antinous in his original cultus had a far wider appeal than is suggested by a survey of the modern cult on the web.[11] The overwhelming modern presentation of this deity as the sole property of gay men places some high obstacles in the path of any woman who might wish to engage with this fascinating and rewarding deity.

The queerness of Antinous is an important aspect of his appeal. Most modern Pagan religions are based in and work from within heteronormative assumptions. Deities and energies are paired off in boy-girl arrangements that, however well intentioned, leave out those of us with non-heterosexual identities. Sexual polarity is presented as the normative driver for much of Neopagan worship and magic. The Antinoan cult provides a strong option for those of us who stand outside this mainstream, provided we wrest it away from exclusivist male claims and their accompanying focus on perfect male youth and beauty.

The very queerness of Antinous and Hadrian themselves, both deities within the cult, provides incredible affirmation for non-heteronormative spirituality. It elevates queer relationship and queer identity from second-class citizenship within Paganism to a primacy of place, celebrating love that looks beyond gender. Yet the Ekklesía does not begin and end with coming out theology. In fact, this has very little to do with the ritual life of the group at all.

In the Ekklesía we embrace not just Antinous and Hadrian but also Hadrian's deified wife, Sabina. Her companion and court poet, Julia Balbilla, is a Sancta of the Ekklesía and their close relationship is specifically constructed as Sapphic in the modern theology of many members of the cult. Antinous himself was closely associated with the goddess Diana in one Roman funeral society,[12] providing concrete proof that there is no hostility between queer male and queer female deities within the cult. Many modern Sancti of the cult are queer women and people of other genders, revered as

---

[10] http://groups.yahoo.com/group/ekklesia_antinoou/
[11] The only love spell invoking Antinous from the ancient world yet found does so to bring about a liaison between a man (the invoker) and a woman (the focus of his desire): Mary Beard, John North, and Simon Price (eds./trans.), *Religions of Rome, Volume 2: A Sourcebook* (Cambridge: Cambridge University Press, 1998), pp. 266-267.
[12] Beard, North, and Price, pp. 292-294.

inspirations, artists, and leaders within the queer community throughout history.

Mantinoe, the mother of Antinous, is also an important figure of deific power.[13] The obelisk of Antinous, originally situated at Hadrian's Villa,[14] says on its north face, "...his mother's whole body heals."[15] This female deific power is certainly worthy of worship and admiration, a fitting attribute for the mother of a god and a goddess in her own right. It is also a feminine deific presence that is not expressed solely within the too-often seen context of woman/goddess/earth as depersonalized passive fertile womb. A whole body is more than a uterus -- it has hands and mouth, brain and eyes. A body has speech and thought and active, motive participation where a womb has only receptive gestation and a cataclysmic expulsion of the finished product.

Hadrian also firmly established the reverence of Disciplina, the feminine embodiment of military discipline, within the Roman legions.[16] Ever a man of philosophy, and one who apparently had a great respect for the women in his life, he was not afraid to represent iron discipline and warriorship as a female figure.

This essay is not, however, solely intended as a discussion of the history of the modern cult of Antinous or an analysis of how deity is understood in the Ekklesía. My intention is to describe my own perceptions and participation within the group. My presence is welcomed and encouraged, yet all too often the group's discussions tend inevitably toward male homosexual-exclusive language. Supposedly inclusive and welcoming video work from members offers welcome and inclusion, but only for gay men.[17] Attention

---

[13] J. R. Rea (ed./trans.), *The Oxyrynchus Papyri*, Vol. 63 (London: Egypt Exploration Society, 1996), pp. 10-11.
[14] Zaccaria Mari and Sergio Sgalambro, "The Antinoeion of Hadrian's Villa: Interpretation and Architectural Reconstruction," *American Journal of Archaeology* 111 (2007), pp. 83-104; Thorsten Opper, *Hadrian: Empire and Conflict* (Cambridge: Harvard University Press, 2008), p. 178.
[15] P. Sufenas Virius Lupus, *The Phillupic Hymns* (Eugene: Bibliotheca Alexandrina, 2008), p. 21. It should additionally be noted that the other Antinoan group leaves this line out of its reading of the obelisk.
[16] Lesley Adkins and Roy A. Adkins, *Dictionary of Roman Religion* (New York: Facts on File, Inc., 1996), p. 63; Anthony R. Birley, *Hadrian the Restless Emperor* (London and New York: Routledge, 2001), pp. 117-120.
[17] http://www.youtube.com/watch?v=ErgRKDi2ots&feature=channel . Note that though the video itself does not claim a unique gay male association for Antinous after its edits, the title of the video certainly seems to indicate such.

called to this exclusivity in one video led to some editing, but the problem remains.

I sometimes find it difficult to achieve visibility within the Ekklesía as a woman, at least in the online discussions. I participate fully in the physical rituals and organization of the group. I engage the group on my own terms as an equal. I have never been overtly dismissed for being female, though when I speak up to widen the discussion to include women I do find that new members are often surprised to find a woman in their midst. Several members of the group, including P. Sufenus Virius Lupus, our most prolific scholar and writer of Antinoan poetics, theology, and ritual, are explicitly welcoming of women, the other-gendered, and non-homosexual men. Our discourse however, by sheer overwhelming numbers, is unfortunately exclusionary.

I have been asked why a woman would want to be in a gay male group and my only answer to that question is that the Ekklesía is not "a gay male group." To quote Lupus, the Ekklesía is a "queer, Graeco-Roman-Egyptian syncretist reconstructionist polytheist form of mystical religion"[18] -- nowhere does the group claim to be for gay men only. In fact, the group's identity is specifically stated to be wider than this. There is one mention of gay culture in the group's description and I can only imagine that this is where seekers get the idea that the Ekklesía is just for gay men.

I have been initiated as a Mystes and acted as a ritualist in initiating others into the mysteries of our worship. Many other women have also participated as "Assistai" (non-initiate ritualists in the mysteries) for the Ekklesía. All of us have found the ritual itself both profound and transformative in its concept and execution. The mysteries are not based on gender or perceptions of gender, nor do they collapse our mystery into the showing of masculine seed that sprouts in female, fertile earth, as was my experience of the modern Eleusinian mysteries. Any role in the mystery, with the possible exception of Antinous himself, may be taken on by a person of any gender or identity. I experienced this as one of the great strengths of the ritual.

In our larger public rituals I have participated as a Luperca, running in the traditional race of the Lupercalia as the first woman to do so in the history of the cult, either in ancient times or in its modern reconstruction. My ritual role was as Luperca Secunda, who

---

[18] http://groups.yahoo.com/group/ekklesia_antinoou/ - group mission statement

represents blood in the ritual. Ironically, I was also menstruating heavily at the time, so blood was present in more than theoretical form. Yet this was not a specific intention of the ritual or the role itself. The blood normally implied is the blood of wounding and battle, given that this was a ritual role that traditionally was reserved for young males entering adulthood. In this case my status as a middle-aged menstruating woman served to turn the tradition entirely on its head and remake it into a much more inclusive symbolic statement.

In 2009 another woman joined me as a Luperca, running the race before nearly a hundred people at PantheaCon in San Jose, California. Given that so far only two public E.A. Lupercalias have been celebrated, this can be considered normative for our large group celebrations, for which I am intensely grateful. It is the stated intention of the group to continue including women as Luperci in these rituals as part of the renewed tradition.

My participation also extends to writing liturgy for the group, specifically constructing ritual for the Lion Hunt and the epiphany of the Lotus, a paired group of rituals acknowledging failures and overcoming them. I expect to write further liturgy as I continue my association with the group, as well. My approach is one emphasizing equality and participation, though the style of Antinoan ritual tends to be more formal than my usual practices outside of that context.

One of the things I find comforting about participation in the E.A. is the fact that I am extremely unlikely ever to find myself unwillingly sexualized as a ritual participant. The focus is never on my body as a vessel of generative femininity or passive receptivity. Creativity is regarded as a given for all participants, and depersonalizing womb imagery is nonexistent. It is this reduction of women to wombs that profoundly disturbs me about my interactions with some women-only Goddess groups. In looking to such groups I would genuinely have expected them to move beyond gender essentialism to embrace all of women's roles and sexualities. Yet even there the goddesses, at least in my experience with such groups, have tended to be expressed either as castrating warriors or as generative wombs. There is little acknowledgment of the scholar, the poet, the builder, the intellectual. Even in specifically women's space, women are reduced to their reproductive capacity.

The triple goddess of Wicca manifesting as maiden, mother, and crone emphasizes childbirth as a defining aspect of womanhood, and one ordinarily can't get to "crone" without passing "mother". To me, this suggests that women who are infertile or those of us who are childless by choice are somehow seen as immature and forever stuck at the maiden stage. This plays an immense role in my appreciation for the cult of Antinous and its lack of emphasis on woman as fertility symbol. My internalized identity as androgynous and my overt bisexuality are respected and embraced within the Ekklesía, where gender and fertility -- male or female -- are not the focus of theology or ritual. As much as women are not reduced to wombs, neither are men reduced to penises and body hair. I find this a distinct improvement over much of modern gender-based Pagan spirituality and its accompanying fertility mysteries.

One aspect of Antinoan theology that is being developed at the moment is a concept of a triad of goddesses of function. Sabina, Hadrian's wife, is the emblem of fidelity. During their long marriage, Sabina never bore children. Despite Hadrian's great love for Antinous, they never divorced even though it was entirely legal and possible for them. Hadrian deified her when she died -- an act that he did not have to perform.[19] There was certainly respect between them, if not love.

Matidia Augusta, the mother of Sabina, and Hadrian's second cousin, represents philosophy. He performed her funeral oration at her death and she was, in fact, the first person he deified as a part of his imperial prerogative.[20] There is a theological assumption within the E.A. that Hadrian's interest in philosophy was pursued with Matidia on some level, given their close friendship.

Julia Balbilla is regarded as a personification of poetry and four of her poems were preserved, engraved upon the Colossus of Memnon during Hadrian's imperial visit to the site after the death of Antinous.[21] The preservation of Julia's poetry is important because it is a recorded woman's poetic voice, praising another woman, with a known authorship and date of inscription during a time when women were largely silent in public.

These roles of fidelity, philosophy, and poetry tend to turn the Neopagan maiden/mother/crone triad on its ear. Matidia, ostensibly the "crone" in her role as Sabina and Hadrian's elder, died

---

[19] Birley, p. 294. A particularly fine relief of Sabina's apotheosis has survived, which is pictured on p. 293.
[20] Birley, pp. 107-113.
[21] André and Étienne Bernand (eds.), *Les Inscriptions Grecques et Latines du Colosse de Memnon* (Paris: Institut Francais d'Archéologie Orientale, 1960), pp. 80-98. A further fragment by Sabina herself follows on pp. 99-100.

at 51, a younger age than either Sabina or Hadrian did. She would certainly be regarded as no more than middle aged today. Sabina, the wife of Hadrian and the one who would normally be placed in a "mother" role as the "consort" of one of the main male deities, had no children. The "maidenly" younger Julia is, as previously noted, constructed as the lover and companion of Sabina. None of these women is presented as a stage of the fertility cycle but all are in relationship to each other and to Hadrian and Antinous. As personifications of admirable concepts often associated with male agency[22], this is an extremely important theological position with wide repercussions for the cult and for Paganism generally.

I would love to see more participation by women in E.A. I feel that the group and Antinous himself have something important to offer and that, for bisexual, lesbian, and androgynous women especially, there can be a genuine non-sexualized model that most mainstream Pagan groups are unable to provide.

References

Lambert, Royston (1996) *Beloved and God: The Story of Hadrian and Antinous.* New York: Zebra.

Biography

Erynn Rowan Laurie is a member of the Ekklesía Antínoou and one of the many founders of the Celtic Reconstructionist Pagan movement. She is the author of *Ogam: Weaving Word Wisdom* and a number of other works. Erynn resides in the Seattle area and partakes of chai at Travelers regularly.

---

[22] Regardless of any cultural attempts to force fidelity upon women, it is considered more of an inborn quality of men. The U.S. Marines motto, "Semper Fidelis" -- "always faithful" -- certainly emphasizes the point.

WHERE DO I GO FROM HERE?
JAYMI ELFORD

Ten years ago, I discovered magic. I sat on the floor at the local Barnes and Noble looking at a three-shelf bookcase full of paperback books and boxes on spells, tarot, and other Wicca-related reading materials. All the shiny spines called out to me. The ones that claimed the knowledge gained from dragons and faeries seemed silly to my uninitiated mind, while the more-gruesome occult-related books by Crowley and other Hermetic magicians just seemed a bit unwieldly. In the end, I selected a rust-colored, slim book on *Tarot Magic by Janina Renee*. Tarot has always intrigued me; I purchased my first deck back in junior high. Seeing that I currently owned a deck, I figured that my first foray into the magical realm should contain elements both familiar and foreign to me.

Two weeks later, a friend and I enrolled in a Basics of Magic class a local pagan/witchy store offered. That's where I discovered how magic has the power to change you and your reality. The class expanded my horizons to the potential of changing my life and I also learned just how deep some scars went in my life. It challenged me to drop many pre-conceived notions of who I was and my rigid perceptions of what the world was and the role I had to play in it. It taught me to trust my intuition and the wisdom of a higher self. For me, magic became a spiritual tool to help me deal with this reality and my manic depression. Six months later, I graduated that class with four others and received my first degree. I then found myself walking down a path as wide open as the world. It was time to find my way and seek out what I could do.

After the class, I hung around the store and its patrons for a few years. I participated in a couple of Samhain rituals, and even took a few more classes and one-on-one trainings. During the summer of 2000 I discovered festivals. That kicked off my love and hate relationship with them. My first festival was held up the Washington State side of the Columbia Gorge. It was a few miles out of town and it seemed like a relatively small and easy one to start out with. Things were going well at the start, but after feeling like my mind was being invaded by several others and just feeling rather down, I left after main ritual without telling anyone. Not the smartest thing I had ever done but I felt like I had to protect myself.

From that experience I learned that I needed to attend festivals and workshops that included a safe and supportive environment. I also learned that as an empath, I needed to be near water so that the sound and the calming energies could wash away all those feelings of being pried into. As a result, my second adventure to the Northwest Fall Equinox Festival was better received. There I fell in love with fire dancing, drumming, and having many wonderful discussions about energy use and tarot with my fellow pagans.

By myself, most of my magical workings revolved around the tarot; stone and crystal lore; and spell working. I created a tarot pathworking book and filled a large, line-bound journal with all my tarot thoughts. It included sections on the cards (with correspondence information), various spreads, spells and rituals, and it even included a whole section on tarot games. While learning more and more about the tarot, I got interested into the Tree of Life. So I pursued knowledge around the sephiroth and the paths and how that interconnected to tarot and our lives. I also wrote spells for various endeavors, held cleansing ceremonies for friends and home, and even celebrated the Sabbats regularly.

The Mono Months

Of course, life gets in the way. Soon I fell into a steady rhythm of the daily grind, work and more work. My job as a website quality assurance technician demanded that I work long and strange hours when sites launched. On the side, as a favor to friends, I helped a small but promising RPG company get their website and online presence going. They relied on my technical abilities as well as my keen observations of technology and user patterns. Soon I found myself providing more information than just a simple designer could offer. As a result of working two full time jobs that fulfilled my passions for both writing and design, I allowed my magical life to slide to the sidelines. However, my witchy thirst for knowledge continued as I read many books and wrote down small observations here and there. I also performed small tarot spells, rituals, and readings, and attended a few psychic fairs to receive some extra cash.

Five years ago, after returning for a trip to California to visit my now-husband, I grew very lethargic. I slept a lot and no matter how much caffeine I guzzled down, nothing touched my body or system. My friends grew worried and at their request I saw my

Where Do I Go From Here?

doctor and had his office test me for mono, Strep, and thyroid issues. I still recall the day my doctor called my office. My boss, George, and I were talking when the phone rang. "You have a textbook case of mono," my doc told me. Inside, I felt like my world had just collapsed in on me— I needed to work. I knew that mono was bad and that it was tough to get over. The look on my boss's face screamed, "go home and sleep and don't come back until your not diseased." But, I feared that by staying home I would have lost my job. Being a single person household meant that no work equaled no ability to pay off bills.

Getting mono was my body's way of telling me to "slow down and look at what you're doing." That is the message that it brought to me, and it was a hard lesson to learn. Working two jobs that wore myself into the ground wasn't healthy at all. At first I tried to keep up my work schedule. I'd go into work and perform my testing tasks to the best of my abilities. But all that did in the end was to wear myself out so much that I'd have to call in sick the next day. After a week of alternating between work and home, my bosses told me to stay home. I ended up using all of my accumulated sick leave (which, at the time was about a month's worth) and tried to enjoy my body's self-imposed vacation.

Mono did a lot to my body. It weakened my immune system, leaving me susceptible to all sorts of secondary sicknesses. Having very little physical energy meant that I couldn't exercise much, or enjoy many of my favorite outdoor activities. As it was summertime, this left me alone, inside, when my friends were out at festivals or camping or hiking. It also meant that my body gained a few extra pounds from the lack of exercise. Mentally, it crushed me. I felt so strange and foreign to myself. All sorts of doubts and fears crept into my mind. As a writer, I found myself lost... unable to tap into my once vast imagination. I lost the ability to dream, and to write my thoughts down. I spent a lot of time picking up books, flipping through the pages, smelling the paper and ink, wishing I could understand the words written down, only to ultimately set them back down again. Reading books and looking at the tarot had become a chore. Instead, I lost myself online. I chatted with friends, surfed the mindless parts of the internet for entertainment, and bought a lot of books through amazon.com; hoping that the day would come when I could read them and add their knowledge to my own. Of course, this was in between sleeping sessions that lasted on the upwards of 20 hours a day.

At one point, I remember trying to raise energy. I was sitting in my bed, feeling frustrated at being constantly tired. Even though I got more than enough sleep, it seemed that it was never enough. I wanted to feel well again and I figured that if I could gather enough energy, then magic could help cleanse me and make the waking nightmare go away faster. I closed my eyes, and imagined my energy — what little I could see and feel within me — and then slowly and cautiously extended it just slightly out into the room. I was hoping that if I could wash myself with this energy, that it could help attack the sickness. But when I went to push it outwards, nothing left. Instead, my breathing was rushed, as if I spent the last short minutes running a marathon. It left me feeling hollow inside. I couldn't keep anything within. I couldn't raise the energy required to do any sort of healing. Healing I so desperately wanted for myself.

The experience left me feeling even more depressed, frustrated and hopelessly trapped inside my own body. Over the next two months my body did win the uphill battle against the mono virus. I thought it was over and that everything would just fall back into place. But what I wasn't expecting was the length of time it took for my energetic/magical body years to recover.

Rebuilding the Magic

For the past three years I felt as if everything I was and knew either stopped existing altogether, or got lost, or had changed into something completely unrecognizable and separate from myself. After I felt "better" I attempted to pick up the pieces of my magical life. I started by testing out the waters with raising energy. Not for anything in particular mind you, just to see if I could fill small room spaces with myself. The harder I pushed, however, the more tired my body grew. During those first months, I discovered that I still lacked the energy to give into magic or meditation. My attempts to meditate were met with me falling asleep. Worse yet, even though I was deemed healthy, I found myself still constantly drained and tired. Staying awake for more than eight hours a day required a nap in between. These naps, then, lasted anywhere between 2-5 hours, depending on whether or not I had to work.

I continued to battle depression. Worried that I would never be able to continue down the magical path I started on before being sick, I sought out answers. I called upon my old friends and told them what happened. Most of my good friends just nodded, sympathized, and stayed silent. They didn't know what to say or offer for advice. I then pushed beyond my immediate community. Once, at a workshop down in Roseburg, Oregon, I met a pagan who had a similar story to mine. She told me that while getting this sick was a horrible, life changing experience, the energy I felt and had was "the will of the universe and that this was all the energy I would probably be able to hold for the rest of my life." She told me I should be thankful that I was left with any and that I should learn to adjust and adapt to this new lifestyle. This answer was something I didn't want to hear. I felt devastated, like my life was over, and that there was no hope of being normal again.

I cried and vowed to continue my search. I refused to believe that a life of minimized energy was all there was left. I wanted was to find a spiritual solution to help raise the quality of life that I felt the mono had stolen from me. I wanted to feel whole again, to be complete, and to raise and hold energy to feel connected to the universe. So I refused to let that be the final answer. I refused to accept that level of energy and pattern of life. While my emotional state kept sinking, my search for a better way continued. I knew that something or someone who could help me was out there.

Two years ago, I met Taylor Ellwood. He, his wife, and myself had been building a friendship. As I was still seeking help for my situation, I popped the "What can I do to get better?" question. Taylor listened patiently to my tale and confirmed my intuition was right— that there was something I could do to get better. He felt as strongly as I that I could regain, rebuild, and overcome the damage the mono did to me magically, and that not only would I be better, but I would surpass where I was before.

We started back at the beginning, with the basics. Our first session evaluated the extent of my issues. Taylor gave me a good look over, psychically. He checked my energetic body and found two large holes hovering over my aura's chest area. This, he suspected, was where the main cause of energy leakage was going on. He then gave me my first Reiki session, and taught me a few breathing exercises: one to help raise energy when I needed it, and another to allow energy to flow out of me. It was this second type of water breathing exercise that became instrumental in rebuilding my magical practice. I left his place that night feeling confident for the first time in three years since being sick that I finally was on the road to recapturing my spiritual practice and myself. At home, I integrated the core exercises into my daily routine. In the morning before doing work, I'd raise energy into my body. This kept the nap monster at bay, giving me countless extra hours to get things done. In the evening, before sleeping, I spent time with water breathing meditation exercise to flow energy over my body. This helped to repair the holes in my aura that constantly leaked energy out.

In just a few short months later, Taylor confirmed that they were gone and I was actually on my way to regaining myself. His teachings taught me how to heal myself. And I reported back the physical changes. I slept less, was able to hold energy, and consequently I felt just happier overall. For the first time in a long time, I felt as if I could once again be apart of magic. He and I continued to work on rebuilding myself, my magical energy and practice. I've been given tips on how to work with the natural universal energy flow, as it flows through us. That it is easier to move with the way it wants to move, rather than trying to push and force it to flow in a way that is not how it wants to move. I've learned more advanced healing techniques that not only help myself, but also allow me to help others, like my husband and other friends.

Once I got the basics down, we added another working to the list of things I could do. We decided to start me out with the year long elemental workings. This is a technique Taylor explains in *Inner Alchemy*, that involves the magician picking an element (it can be one of the standard five or creating one of your own) and a patron deity (again, this is traditional or not) and then spending a whole year working with that element. I selected the element of movement as my first attempt, and partnered with Lance Armstrong as the patron deity. In that year, not only did I find that my energy and breathing helped move me but I also kept to a rigorous exercise schedule that also helped boost my ability to retain energy and keep me going throughout the day. I started my next element, acceptance, in June of 2009.

Even today, I'm still in the midst of recapturing and rebooting my magical practice. My journey into magic has taken me another five years to develop. But with my energetic body still healing and growing, I know there is no fast track to this process. I take it slowly, one thing at a time. For the first time in my life, I know and feel that anything is possible for me again when it comes to magic and learning and experiencing it. It's not always shiny or happy, but I really do believe that this is a hurdle that can be overcome. Some days the frustration and anxiety wash over me and I feel as if I have not moved further than being able to do anything but my breathing exercises. That my mind is not as focused as it used to be and I don't always feel connected to my passions and the things that I used to and still define myself by. On those days, I slide and beat myself up, but I never give into the darkness. I recognize it as part of the process and I continue on. I know that one day the image of myself inside my mind will manifest itself on the outside as well.

So where do I go from here? I feel like there's no real ending to this but just more path to follow and explore. Then again, isn't life more about the journey and not the destination?

These days I view myself continuing the rebuilding phase of my practice. I still read a lot of books. I'm not sure if I want to stay "solitary" or if I want to participate in a coven or tradition; but I have been talking with friends who are in various covens to see what their perspectives are. I'm involved in several endeavors, all which give me new ways to reconnect and explore opportunities that I'm passionate about. These include, performing experimental magic with Taylor and others. I've enrolled myself in The Tarot School's Tarot Degree Program because I want to solidify my tarot training. One day, I hope to teach tarot to others in workshops, podcasts, and in-person classes. I'm also working with friends on redefining what magic means to me; relearning the basics of grounding, centering, and shielding and exploring how I want magic to affect change in my life. I am also actively participating in festivals and rituals once more and enjoying it immensely.

Biography

Jaymi Elford believes that magic is a path one walks on, as well as a tool to help explore the world we live in. She's two months into her elemental work with acceptance and talks to AFP, the element's deity, on a daily basis. If you happen to spot her sometime, feel free to cheer her on and share your experiences. Jaymi lives in the Pacific Northwest with her loving husband, 3 cats, and an ever growing collection of books. You can find her online at www.shadesofmaybe.com (personal domain) and at www.diyplanner.com (articles on creativity, journalling, and reviews).

THE FEMINIST ADEPT
BRANDY WILLIAMS

I have been a feminist and a magician since my late teens, three and a half decades now. My feminist self and my magical self haven't always worked together. These two aspects of my identity/work came together at two major points in my life.

Feminist Qabalist Collective

The typed letter came without warning and launched directly into its purpose.

> **May Day, 1985:**
>
> > Dear Brandy,
> >
> > This is your invitation to participate in a feminist collective for the purpose of re/searching the Hermetic traditions, re/claiming and acknowledging wimmin's contributions in magic(k), and bringing forth a non-sexist context in which to develop as magic(k)al people...
> >
> > Phase Two of the collective will be to co-write a book, with the proposed title of The Feminist Adept.

The dozen or so women and men in the Feminist Qabalist Collective spanned the globe. We communicated in pre-internet days through early expensive copiers, automatic typewriters, mainframe computer printouts, mimeograph, and handwritten letters. The collective wrote in the feminist language of the time - wimmin, re/claiming. It was, in the grand tradition of feminist collectives, spectacularly radical. For a period of a year or so I was encouraged to share my thinking, to be bold and courageous, to dare to overturn thousands of years of oppressive philosophy, to speak my own experience and turn that experience into ritual that others could perform.

The Feminist Adept

The group faithfully followed the life arc of an 80's collective: initial enthusiasm, fierce discussion, discovery of fundamental incompatibilities, and ultimate disbandment. These people had come together through the small press community, and none were physically near me or personal friends, so when the group ceased to circulate ideas I lost contact with all of its members.

The group left an indelible mark. In many ways I am still a Feminist Qabbalist, member of a group that no longer exists, but stubbornly loyal to its ideals. In the years since the collective disbanded I have held the idea in the back of my mind that someday I would write that book.

Intermission: Suspension of Belief

When the collective stopped working it was clear to me that I needed to do my homework in the magical fields. As the youngest and least experienced member of the group the communal discussion often left me behind. I spent decades studying traditional Witchcraft and Qabbalah. Because of my initial work in feminist Qabbalah I noted some issues as I went along, but I set them aside for the moment. With that marvelous esoteric trick of mind, the ability to hold more than one truth at once, I neither believed nor disbelieved any particular dogma. I treated each principle as true within its own system. This by the way deeply offends those people whose worldview is dependent on the concept of absolute truth ("God/Gardner/Crowley said it, I believe it, that settles it.") In order to advance in my magical practice I set aside my feminist observations and concerns.

Feminist Thelema

About twenty years later, two higher-ranking men who had sponsored me to an O.T.O. initiation took me out to dinner after the initiation. They asked me, "Why do people think the O.T.O. isn't feminist?" I thought, oh my gosh, they actually don't *know*.

It was time to stop setting aside my feminist instincts. With twenty years of magical practice I now had the knowledge I had lacked during the collective's days. I needed to brush up on my feminism though - I had dropped out of active involvement with feminist movement in the late 70s when it took that regrettable sex negative turn.

First I revisited feminist literature to get back up to speed on the current state of the movement. Since Robin Morgan's anthology *Sisterhood is Powerful* had been so important to me in my young adulthood it was exciting to pick up *Sisterhood is Forever*, and a mortality check to realize it had been thirty years since her first book. The book led me on to others (in the humanist studies branching tree model of research) that kept me happily reading for several years. I found that feminist movement in the early 2000s was battered from two decades of backlash but stubbornly persisting in its goals. The movement is a lot more sophisticated about race, culture, and gender than it was in the 70s, but is still inexplicably at odds with the sex positive movement.

I read an entire shelf of books of feminist theology in the world's religions. The Christian feminists seemed to have gotten the farthest in rethinking the theology of their religion. I aspire to Sister Elizabeth Johnson's bravery in her discussion of the Pope's refusal to consider ordination of women: "I get the impression that the recourse to sheer power is happening because those who oppose women's ordination are losing the argument on the field of reasoning" (Johnson 1996).

I thrilled to Rita Gross' critiques of androcentric scholarship in *Feminism and Religion* (Gross 1996) and her specific application of that critique to Buddhism: "In other words, to be true to its own vision, Buddhism needs to transcend its androcentrism and patriarchy." (Gross 1993.) It was the greatest affirmation to meet Irshad Manji in person, a woman living under threat of death since writing *The Trouble with Islam Today* (Manji 2005), and have her take my hand and tell me to continue to do my work. She urged me to understand that in a free society there is no reason for self-censorship.

Immersed in these theological discussions I felt part of a greater community of women questioning our given faiths and working to expand our understanding of the universe to include the insights of women. Buoyed by this sense of community I wrote the first draft of "Feminist Thelema." I presented it with some apprehension and was pleased that I was not immediately run off the podium. I ended the presentation with a discussion session. That discussion fed into the next version of the paper which I wrote and presented. This process of discussion and refinement went on for several years. Toward the end of the process I presented at a national ceremonial conference, then a national Pagan conference. I finalized the paper and put it up on the web.

The Feminist Adept

"Feminist Thelema" presents a gender analysis of Thelema, from social, theological, and philosophical points of view. It isn't *The Feminist Adept*, but it does lay the groundwork for further exploration, and the basis of the work is the impact the Feminist Qabbalist Collective had on me a couple of decades ago.

It was received surprisingly well. I was given space to present and was published. Thoughtful people engaged me in thoughtful conversation about my points. Eventually of course backlash developed. Backlash technically seeks to preserve a status quo. Backlash is what happened to feminist movement, which hit a high water mark in the mid-80s and then fought the current for two decades to hang onto those gains. Backlash is always successful because it diverts energy from change into preservation.

I wouldn't have been able to handle the initial backlash in my somewhat less confident youth, but I'm no longer young or so easy to push around, and the sense of community with other feminist theologians and philosophers gave me the courage to deal with it for a period of time. I also found surprising sympathy and support among ceremonial men - when some men banded together to front the usual "feminism is stupid" critiques, other men defended my space to speak.

The backlash that finally stopped the work for me was the commentary that developed among my sisters. Women in traditional magical communities directly acted to block my access to information, to reject proposals to speak, to frame my experience as personal issues rather than indications of problems in the magical systems, and to reject my offer of feminist sisterhood.

Each incident was isolated and had no reference to any other. On each occasion I would stop, cry, and reassess whether I had the courage to continue. When I blogged about this experience my sisters in the magical communities were genuinely aghast. Women who are not feminist wrote and called to let me know they cared about my ability to work and about how I felt. It was as much to ease their distress as to ease my own that I stopped presenting on the topic of feminist Thelema.

Traditional Women's Culture

At that moment of discouragement I dug out the old Feminist Qabbalist Collective letters and re-read them, to try to recapture what it felt like when I was encouraged to question, to explore, to challenge orthodoxy. When I wasn't the most radical woman magician I knew.

I spent some time confused, frustrated, and silenced. I had fallen through the crack between woman and feminist. As a feminist I understand that the personal is the political - what happens to any of us can happen to all of us, not because of our individual shortcomings, but because of institutional inequities. As a feminist I am also highly sensitive to the unique individuality of each woman, how important it is to honor the differences in our work, not to impose an interpretation or to appropriate the meaning of that work. The woman biographer of a woman magician may bring no feminist intent to that work, so I might point to that work as contributing to women's history, but I am careful not to label the work feminist. As a feminist I wish for all women to have a space to contribute, whether that woman is feminist or not.

Whether that woman is feminist or not turns out to be a pretty good indicator of whether or not the woman will reciprocate that sense of respect. Fighting the ingrained sexism in traditional magic I needed support from other women. What I was getting was slapped down.

Traditional women's culture both supports and suppresses women's work. Women's language emphasizes the connection between women, and that serves to provide emotional support for our work, up to a certain point. However, traditional women's culture does not permit women to achieve. Tannen pointed to this aspect of women's culture: "Appearing better than others is a violation of the girls' egalitatian ethic: People are supposed to stress their connections and similarities" (Tannen 1990).

The dominant culture requires women to serve the needs of men. Women do the housework, are available sexually when wanted, bear and raise the children, support men emotionally. The dominant culture requires women to cede the speaking floor/job/living wage to men, not to brag about our accomplishments but to minimize them, to adapt to men's norms, and not to challenge the dominance heirarchy.

At present the dominant culture allots about ten percent of living wage jobs to women. This places half the population in competition for a very limited resource, while the other half competes for the remaining ninety percent. Women who win one of these coveted positions, as I have, may find ourselves working in isolation from other women - at business meetings I am often the only woman in the room.

Patriarchal culture places women in competition with one another in other ways, most notably competing with one another for the protection of a particular man. Young sexually attractive women can gain significant concessions from men, which is a form of power, and in some cases may be a woman's only power. Trading on sexual attractiveness to men is a young woman's game - past menopause women become much less sexually attractive to men, a fact which sometimes frightens younger women, who may find this very difficult to face or discuss.

Traditional women's culture acts to support the dominant culture. A woman who is seeking recognition for her individual accomplishments or who challenges the dominance heirarchy may be punished by both the dominant culture and traditional women's culture. Women who have achieved a position in a male-dominated field or who have established a relationship with a man of status may reject the company of other women as potential competitors. The generational divide also opens - younger women may refuse to talk to older women about their post-sexual-power experiences, while older women may suppress younger women's attempts to change traditional women's culture.

The mechanisms traditional women's culture uses to bring women into line are criticism and ostracization - aggressive critique which may be intended and received as attacking, framing the woman's issues as personal rather than systemic, and ultimately refusing to enter into relationship with the woman at all, freezing her out of the group.

Women hurt women, and this is how. Women betray women. Mothers raise daughters into traditional women's culture, which ranks women's needs as secondary to the needs of the men they serve. (My mother taught me always to serve the men at the table first.) Women who have achieved positions of power refuse to aid less powerful women who ask for assistance. Friends criticise one another and refuse to provide each other with emotional support.

It should not have come as a surprise to me that women in traditional magical groups would act in the same ways as women in other traditional cultures. Traditional magical women may act to protect the position of being a singular woman in a male dominated group, trade on the sexuality which some groups emphasize as women's most important power, critique and suppress challenges to the established heirarchy, and fail to respond to the pain and requests for support of the women around them. Also, women who have invested years or lives into a system may find it difficult to understand challenges to that system - it may feel personal to them, as if they themselves are under attack.

I didn't know how to talk about this. Even bringing up the issue felt as if it was itself a criticism and a betrayal. I ended up isolated, hurt, and alone.

Collective Genius

My personal experience bore out what my reading was telling me. Women need groups around us to support us. One reason of course is that the culture itself is set up to promote men and to ignore women's accomplishments. As Christine Battersby explored in detail in *Gender and Genius* (Battersby 1989), the Western concept of genius valorizes a brilliant man integrating his feminine side. By definition women can't be geniuses, only muses. Women need the support of other women just to be able to be recognized for our work at all.

The four women who wrote *Women's Ways of Knowing* composed the book in a collective style to reflect their findings that women's work blossoms in a community setting. Women, they said, develop a sense of self through questioning received authority and recognizing the equal importance of our individual experience. Men and women both develop the tools of reason and analysis. Women tend to use reason and analysis to relate to the work of others around us - we check our conclusions by sharing them with others, and evaluate the impact of our work on our communities.

Still isolated and hurt, I longed to apply these lessons to the task of building women's magical community. I wrote this manifesto:

> I want my sisters to understand that sisterhood is powerful. I want us to relate to each other not just through the magical men around us but directly woman to woman. I want us to have places where we meet with no men in the room or authorizing the meeting, true woman-only spaces. I want those spaces to at least accommodate feminist discussion. I want a magical woman's culture that doesn't insist I identify with the Divine Feminine (as the unmanifest aspect of the Divine which is only fully embodied by men). I want to challenge men's norms, and I want to do it in the company of other women. I want women more powerful than me to support my work, and

The Feminist Adept

women less powerful than me to ask me for my support. I want us to take each other seriously, to critique each other's work fairly, and from the point of view of supporting our ability to engage in our work. I want to achieve works of genius and be cheered for it. I want to take turns with other women achieving works of genius and cheering them for it.

No sooner had I typed this manifesto than it invoked the result I had called for. Literally hours after I finalized it my cell phone rang. A sister was challenging traditional magical culture and reached out to me for my emotional support. That opened the lines of communication again, and days later I found myself talking with a group of my sisters about these experiences. Not only did these women give me what I had longed for - woman to woman, feminist, magical discussion - they also gave me the critique that I needed. They let me know that if I stop speaking I not only silence my own voice, but also withdraw the support that others need. They reminded me what Irshad Manji had said to me: *in a free society there is no reason for self-censorship*. They challenged me to stop waiting for someone more powerful than me to give me permission to do my work, but instead to just go ahead and do it.

The fundamental feminist act is to contest privilege in ourselves and in the world. Contesting privilege in ourselves humbles us and inspires us to act compassionately. Contesting privilege in the world teaches us the need to reach out to our sisters. I have come to understand that women who have not contested privilege in ourselves do not have the knowledge or empathy to genuinely support other women. By the same token feminism actively requires us to reach out to the women around us, to offer our time, our empathetic ear, and our hand to help each other in the work, to create a space for our sisters to do whatever we need to do.

When I isolated myself from my magical community, I knew that that the feminist adept cannot work alone. My sisters have challenged me to recognize that no one has the power to stop my work except myself. So long as I keep speaking my sisters will listen and answer. I may have to be the first to make the change that I want to see in the world, but as long as I keep speaking, I will not be the last.

References

Battersby, Christine (1989). *Gender and Genius, Towards a Feminist Aesthetics*. Bloomington: Indiana University Press.

Belenky, Mary Field, Blythe McVicker Clinchy, Nancy Rule Goldberger and Jill Mattuckc Tarule (1986, 1997). *Women's Ways of Knowing, The Development of Self, Voice and Mind*. New York: Basic Books.

Morgan, Robin, ed. (2003). *Sisterhood is Forever: The Women's Anthology for a New Millenium*. New York: Washington Square Press.

Gross, Rita (1993). Buddhism After Patriarchy, A Feminist History, Analysis, and Reconstruction of Buddhism. New York: State University of New York Press.

(1996) Feminist and Religion, An Introduction. Boston: Beacon Press.

Johnson, Elizabeth A. 'Disputed questions: authority, priesthood, women.' *Commonweal*, vol.123, January 26 1996

Manji, Urshad (2005). *The Trouble with Islam Today, A Muslim's Call for REform in Her Faith*. New York: St. Martin's Press.

Biography

Brandy Williams is past master of Vortex Oasis of the Ordo Templi Orientis and an ordained priestess of Ecclesia Gnostica Catholica. She is a member of Temple of Light and Darkness, a group in the tradition of the Open Source Order of the Golden Dawn. She is also a founding member of the Coven of the Mystical Merkabah, a coven which is a twenty-year member of the Covenant of the Goddess, and is a former national president of COG.

Brandy's books include *Ecstatic Ritual, Practical Sex Magic*, Megalithica Books, and *Practical Magic for Beginners*, Llewellyn. The version of "Feminist Thelema" presented at NOTOCON 2007 has been printed in *Beauty and Strength, Proceedings of the Sixth Biennial National Ordo Templi Orientis Conference*, United States Grand Lodge, Ordo Templi Orientis, 2009. Her next book-length project has the working title *The Woman Magician*.

THREE CHAPTERS FROM A MAGICAL LIFE
MORDANT CARNIVAL

Preamble

I want to be clear from the outset that my view of gender is that while "biology is not destiny," and which traits and forms of expression are deemed "male" and "female" is largely a matter of culture, the experience of gender—the sense of being male or female oneself—is very real. I'm also okay with the idea that at least some traits generally tend to be commoner in women than men, and vice versa, although when it comes to individuals all bets are off.

It's also reasonable to acknowledge the historical gendering of certain traits and skill-sets. It would be absurd to try and retcon pre-Christian cultures into egalitarian wonderlands—just as it would be completely irrational to try and insist that everyone try to readopt those roles. Every individual has to work out how they're going to respond to that, and find a workable balance.

1: Pagan

Sexist attitudes seem to have become ingrained at a very basic level, in the concepts which are presented as the foundation blocks of magic, specifically the idea of 'male' and 'female' as the active force and the passive vessel respectively. This feeds into the various roles ascribed to male and female magicians. Even in spaces where the female is valorised, this model can often persist unexamined. All that changes is that supposedly feminine qualities are lauded over supposedly male ones.

I virtually stopped going to pagan and magical gatherings until I was in my 30s. In my younger days they were just too much effort.

Some men were supportive and I enjoyed their company. Some women were friendly and I felt we had something to offer each other. But I rapidly got sick of the same issues cropping up and needing to be handled: not just guys who were inappropriate in obvious, or even more subtle ways, or the pretty henna-haired girlfriend looking daggers at you over her partner's shoulder rather than interacting with you because she saw you as a threat, but simply feeling at odds with prevailing expectations. I initially looked into Goddess-based paths but found myself unsatisfied with that approach; it never felt quite right. I simply could not *get into* being female, invest in femaleness as a magical and spiritual state. The magical feminine as outlined in countless texts—passive, receptive, emotive, non-rational—didn't feel like who I was. At the same time I was fiercely at odds with the physicality of my female embodiment. Things like my monthly bleed; so happily celebrated as a connection to the Moon and a time of especial empowerment, this was mostly a source of inconvenience and pain for me. I did not at the time understand why that might be.

There were other obstacles to face-to-face interaction, of course—my own low social skills didn't help. But the assumptions, the expectations, the thousand unwritten rules I always seemed to be transgressing—it was so exhausting, so disheartening, and so relentlessly uninspiring that I eventually just gave up. I did eventually find magical, occult and pagan communities I could gel with, but it took a long time.

In neo-pagan contexts, you're handed this very limited range of possible roles. You can be some variant on the Maiden, Mother or Crone. Too much variance is parsed as either extraneous material to be ignored or ditched, a sign of mundanity, ignorance, or outright perversion. Instead of opening the mind to the possibilities presented by such archetypal figures, they become limiting; all that diversity of expression and experience is stripped or crushed. Some women really blossom in those roles, being attuned to them; but what often happens is that other ways of being female get squeezed out.

2: Chaos Magician

I never really connected with any neo-pagan path, and in my mid-twenties found myself gravitating towards chaos magic.

Chaos magic is hard to define, but could loosely be described as a metamagical system relying on the idea that belief is a tool, and belief systems are something to be picked up and set down at will. This appealed to my scepticism, the part of me that was uncomfortable with the apparently acausal nature of magic and the dimly-explored nature of Gods and spirits. In the context of chaos magic, it is perfectly acceptable to adopt an extreme form of the psychology model, wherein ritual is a sophisticated way of focusing the subconscious on a life-goal rather than a way of literally altering reality. Although I moved away from this pared-down version of magic and into something that would at least admit of magical effects that were not explicable by science, I pursued a non-theistic path for many years. I was enchanted by the freedom offered by the chaos paradigm: the detachment from worn-out ideas and dogma. The possibilities made me feel almost weightless.

But when it came to interacting with other people involved in chaos magic I found myself up against the same kinds of prejudice, manifesting as less easily-defined issues relating to magic as a vehicle for personal freedom. This is at the center of a lot of modern magical discourse involving chaos and post-chaos practitioners, and it doesn't look like being resolved any time soon. It's related to certain strains of political thought, the most extreme example of which would be "manarchism"--anarchism coloured by masculinist and macho attitudes, often with little examination to underpin them. Many magical practitioners are working from the assumption that personal freedom must necessarily include the freedom to dismiss and denigrate others on the grounds of gender, without having to examine such attitudes or back them up with real evidence; the concept of feminism and sexual equality as being, in some never-adequately-explored sense, oppressive. In magical spaces, this seems to manifest in a model of magic as something primarily done by men, with women playing a supporting role--or no role at all beyond being the unwitting target of a working to get into your knickers.

Jake Horsely's pop magic Matrix cash-in, "Matrix Warrior," provides the following summation of this position (and yes, he's entirely serious here):

> "...men have become mincing sissies, ineffective and impotent, and females (in consequence) are sexually unsatisfied harpies from Hell. The solution, then, is for Man to regain his lusty, Pan-like nature as a dominant sexual being, and for Woman to inherit her power as a sexually voracious receptacle of the god-current, or Phallus."

Unless you crib your world-view from colour-supplements, you will recognise this to be nonsense. The idea that men have all been brainwashed to become "mincing sissies" is laughable. Sexism and pointless machismo are in pretty good shape. Society may have grudgingly made room for a greater variety of gender expression but generally it is still very much restricted, with both "sissies" and "harpies" being subject to social sanctions for their transgressive behaviour—including beatings and death.

This kind of comment represents a demand for the advances that have been made in equality to be thrown to the winds. Everyone must jettison their own ideas of who they are, and jump without thought into rigidly stereotyped gender roles. If you're female, this means that you must be a "voracious receptacle." You must give up all thought of an identity other than as Vessel for the real magic: the God-current possessed only by males. This will of course be best expressed through your willingness to spread your legs.

The idea that to express our "true will" we really need a sturdier patriarchy is the worst kind of oppressive tripe. Yet it is a concept with an enormous amount of currency.

3: Heathen

After nine or ten years as a chaos magician, I had a religious experience with the God Loki which resulted in my conversion to heathenry. This path fulfils me in ways that the less rigorous world of neo-paganism never did. I love my Gods, I love the spirits who have come into my life, and I love the communities I've found through heathenry.

However, I've also found that entering into heathen circles has brought its own challenges. There's a strong emphasis in many groups on polarised gender roles. To be fair there is a solid body of lore supporting a division of "male" and "female" in the day-to-day life of pre-Christian heathens. But some groups and individuals take the idea to a ridiculous degree—one group I know of actually forbids its women to even touch weaponry, a prohibition not supported historically or in lore. Although most groups don't take things so far, there's a kind of misty-eyed yearning towards an imagined golden age where Men Were Real Men And Women Knew Their Place.

This is neither appropriate for the modern era nor supported historically. In medieval Europe, pre-Christian heathen women enjoyed an almost unparalleled degree of social and political freedom. The myths and legends of the Northern tradition blossom with powerful female figures: wise Goddesses, warlike Valkyries, strong human heroines. Women were seen as being possessed of magical power, insight, and foresightedness. There are also tantalising hints of meaningful social roles for non-gender-conforming people: suggestions of cross-dressing for magical and spiritual purposes, and other intriguing ideas. Archaeological evidence also supports the idea that some women fought as warriors.

The Future

As well as showing me to my proper spiritual path, Loki revealed other truths to me. One is that while I might be embodied as a female, I'm not a "woman." After decades of struggling to accept and adapt to a female identity, I finally gave in and began to identify as third-gendered. The realisation was like laying down a huge weight. I've got an even bigger fight on my hands now than I did as a woman, but it's one I'm ready for.

Biography

Mordant Carnival has been practicing various forms of magic and divination since childhood. A heathen and dedicated Lokean, hir magicoreligious practice centers around ancestor veneration and the the worship of the land spirits, as well as the Gods of the North. Ze engages in various forms of folk and urban magic, and is very active in the group of ecstatic bodymind practices known as Somafera.

CONCLUSION

In a way this anthology grew out of a paper I wrote, "Feminist Thelema." Taylor Ellwood read the paper and *got it*. He offered me the opportunity to edit an anthology of women's work in magical fields where we are less visible than we are in Pagan or Wiccan communities. I jumped at the chance to act out my principles. I remain enormously grateful to him for his belief in me and in the process.

I wrote the introduction as a response to the many women who emailed me asking me what I wanted. Was I looking for academic work or stories? Work from a particular community? The underlying question seemed to me to be, "Is it okay for me to say this?" I needed to articulate what I was thinking, where I was coming from, to provide an example and a starting point. I wanted to give contributors permission and encouragement to speak in their own voices and in their own styles.

I wanted to assure women that it wasn't necessary to be feminist to contribute to the book. I am very sensitive to the appropriation of women's work into the work of others. These women aren't doing anyone's work but their own. I didn't want to claim any particular work in any way, I wanted to give it the space to be whatever it genuinely is. I will admit that the overtly feminist work submitted by some contributors was thrilling to me. While individual contributors each have their own perspective and right to self-definition, the desire to give them the space to contribute here derives from my feminist ideals.

Listening to these voices was a moving experience. I cheered, I laughed, I cried. I pumped my fist in the air and shouted "Yes!" Some of the pieces were difficult to read, not because of writing skill or content, but because the stories were so raw and moving. I know how hard it is to find time to write in our busy schedules, and each of these pieces was carved out of lives that have little time in them for any extraneous work. I am deeply grateful for the time, effort, and willingness to share that each contributor brought to the work.

Some of the pieces came through in their final form. Others required some feedback. In each case I strove to make suggestions for clarity without imposing a voice on the contributor. As a feminist I consciously worked to stay clean in the work, to keep myself out of it, and to help the woman say most clearly the thing she wanted to say.

My dearest wish would be to bring these women together in a room. Toward the end of the process I found myself saying to them, "You will really like this other piece that has been contributed." I think sisters will find each other through this volume.

That is not to say that their work creates a coherent whole or a new form of magic. If it did I would have failed in the goal to create a collective space for individual achievement. Each of us can take a unique approach to our work, while still learning from one another, and encouraging each other to keep on doing the work. I hope that through this work other women, and people of all genders, will find renewed energy to pursue their own unique magical paths. Then, as Soror Inde Seraphina says, "please write an essay about it, so we can continue to learn from each other as women and magicians."

The end of the anthology is the beginning of the conversation.

Brandy Williams

Three Chapters from a Magical Life

Brandy Williams

DID YOU LIKE WHAT YOU READ?

Ecstatic Ritual by Brandy Williams
978-1-905713-25-7/MB0111
$21.99/£12.99 paperback
Sex magic from a woman's perspective; introduces basic concepts, as well as more advanced material accessible to women of all sexualities.

Ogam: Weaving Word Wisdom by Erynn Rowan Laurie
ISBN 978-1-905713-02-8 /MB0110
$21.99/£12.99 paperback
Ogam isn't just about divination and trees—it's a complex magical symbol system. This well-received text will guide you through the origin, meanings, and practical applications of ogam.

Raising Hell: Subversive Spirituality, Insurrectionist Witchcraft and Black Magic by Kali Black
ISBN 978-1905713-38-7/ MB0135
$20.99/£12.99 paperback
Raising Hell asks what black magic really is and offers a subversive perspective on why magic is done and what it should be done for, how we can be socially responsible in how we practice magic, while also questioning what power really is, and how we manifest or don't manifest that power with our magical practice.

DIY Totemism: Your Personal Guide to Animal Totems by Lupa
ISBN 978-1905713-19-6 / MB0118
$21.99/£12.99 paperback
Tired of totem animal dictionaries? Write your own! Lupa shows you how to create personalized relationships with any animal totem out there, without relying on hackneyed formulae and cultural appropriation.

FIND THESE AND THE REST OF OUR CURRENT LINEUP AT
HTTP://WWW.IMMANION-PRESS.COM

www.ingramcontent.com/pod-product-compliance
Ingram Content Group UK Ltd.
Pitfield, Milton Keynes, MK11 3LW, UK
UKHW041417180426
11947UKWH00007B/178